Social Issues
in Literature

Politics in George
Orwell's *Animal Farm*

Other Books in the Social Issues in Literature Series:

Social Issues
in Literature

Politics in George
Orwell's *Animal Farm*

Dedria Bryfonski, Book Editor

GREENHAVEN PRESS
A part of Gale, Cengage Learning

New Lenox
Public Library District
120 Veterans Parkway
New Lenox, Illinois 60451

GALE
CENGAGE Learning™

Detroit • New York • San Francisco • New Haven, Conn • Waterville, Maine • London

Christine Nasso, *Publisher*
Elizabeth Des Chenes, *Managing Editor*

© 2011 Greenhaven Press, a part of Gale, Cengage Learning

Gale and Greenhaven Press are registered trademarks used herein under license.

For more information, contact:
Greenhaven Press
27500 Drake Rd.
Farmington Hills, MI 48331-3535
Or you can visit our Internet site at gale.cengage.com

For product information and technology assistance, contact us at

Gale Customer Support, 1-800-877-4253
For permission to use material from this text or product, submit all requests online at www.cengage.com/permissions

Further permissions questions can be emailed to permissionrequest@cengage.com

Articles in Greenhaven Press anthologies are often edited for length to meet page require-ments. In addition, original titles of these works are changed to clearly present the main thesis and to explicitly indicate the author's opinion. Every effort is made to ensure that Greenhaven Press accurately reflects the original intent of the authors. Every effort has been made to trace the owners of copyrighted material.

Cover image © Bettmann/Corbis.

LIBRARY OF CONGRESS CATALOGING-IN-PUBLICATION DATA

Politics in George Orwell's Animal farm / Dedria Bryfonski, book editor.
        p. cm. -- (Social issues in literature)
    Includes bibliographical references and index.
    ISBN 978-0-7377-5020-1 -- ISBN 978-0-7377-5021-8 (pbk.)
    1. Orwell, George, 1903-1950. Animal farm. 2. Political fiction, English--History and criticism. 3. Politics in literature. I. Bryfonski, Dedria.
    PR6029.R8A763 2010
    823'.912--dc22
                                                                    2010019306

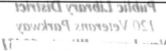

Printed in the United States of America
1 2 3 4 5 6 7 14 13 12 11 10

Contents

Chapter 1: Background on George Orwell

Contemporary Authors

An ardent proponent of human decency, individuality, and social welfare, Orwell was also a foe of such ideological mass movements as fascism and communism. In his masterworks, *Animal Farm* and *Nineteen Eighty-Four*, he warned of the threat to human liberty posed by the growing power of government.

George Orwell

In this rediscovered preface to *Animal Farm*, Orwell writes of the difficulty of getting the book published due to an unwillingness of British publishers and intellectuals to offend the Soviet Union, which was at that time an ally in World War II. Orwell notes that the principle of freedom of the press is violated by this form of censorship, which has no place in a democracy.

John P. Rossi

An overriding concern of Orwell's, best expressed in *Nineteen Eighty-Four* and *Animal Farm*, was the way governments of any type can become totalitarian by a disregard for truth and a corruption of language. These concerns remain relevant in the twenty-first century.

Chapter 2: Politics in *Animal Farm*

Introduction

The twenty-first-century student reading *Animal Farm* encounters a challenge not present to earlier generations of readers: The country satirized in the book—the Soviet Union, or USSR—was dissolved in 1991. At the turn of the twenty-first century, communism, the political system that is satirized, was in power in only five of the world's countries. If the book were only a diatribe against an enemy who is no longer a threat, its relevance would be diminished today. Despite its apparent simplicity as an animal fable, however, *Animal Farm* is an intricate book, and knowledge of the historical context behind the book is helpful in understanding its complexities.

In particular, an understanding of the context is important in comprehending why Orwell—an established author—had a difficult time getting *Animal Farm* published. His native Great Britain has a long history of freedom of the press and is considered the birthplace of freedom of expression; yet the subject matter of *Animal Farm* caused more than twenty publishers to turn down the novel before it was finally accepted by Secker & Warburg.

Orwell knew that he would have difficulty getting *Animal Farm* published. He was under contract to Victor Gollancz, but before sending the manuscript for *Animal Farm*, he wrote a letter saying, "I must tell you that it is—I think—completely unacceptable politically from your point of view (it is anti-Stalin)." Orwell's prediction was on the mark—Gollancz was the first of many publishers to turn down the book. Jonathan Cape was enthusiastic about publishing *Animal Farm* but took the step of sending the manuscript to the UK Ministry of Information as "a matter of policy." An official at the ministry wrote a letter imploring Jonathan Cape not to publish a book that would be so damaging to the country's relations with the Soviet Union. Cape responded to Orwell that "my reading of the manuscript gave me considerable personal enjoyment and satisfaction," but "I can see now that it might be regarded as something which it was highly ill-advised to publish at the present time." In his suppressed preface to *Animal Farm*, later published as "The Freedom of the Press" in *New Statesman and Society*, Orwell commented on the tenor of the times, saying, "Hardly anyone will print an attack on [Soviet leader Joseph] Stalin, but it is quite safe to attack [British prime minister Winston] Churchill, at any rate in books and periodicals."

It is difficult to understand how this level of censorship could exist in the democracy that was Great Britain in the twentieth century. Again, an understanding of events at the time is illuminating.

Although the Soviet Union had signed a nonaggression pact with Germany and intended to stay out of World War II, Adolf Hitler betrayed the pact and attacked the USSR in June 1941. Hitler wanted to stop the spread of communism, gain additional resources for his war effort, and eliminate the Soviet Union as a military power. In reality, he brought into the war a foe that would fiercely and punishingly fight his troops.

The entrance of the Soviet Union into the war as a member of the Allies was a tremendous boon to Great Britain, France, and the other Allied nations. The war was not progressing well for the Allied Forces. France had been taken over by the Germans in June 1940 and was an occupied country. The German Luftwaffe (air force) was waging an air assault on England, with regular bombing raids on London. Pearl Harbor in Hawaii had not yet been bombed, and the United States was still a neutral nation. The entrance of the Soviet Union boosted the Allies because it divided the German forces, who now had to fight in both eastern and western Europe.

Orwell started writing *Animal Farm* in November 1943 and completed it in February 1944, when he began his search for a publisher. At this point, the Soviet Union was fiercely battling the Nazi enemy, and it was considered impolitic to criticize this staunch ally. At the war's end, Soviet deaths would total 27 million, almost half of the 60 million total. For most of the media, the Soviet war effort far overshadowed the atrocities committed by Stalin. Looking back in 2008, the British Broadcasting Corporation (BBC) declared the news media "rosy-eyed" in their treatment of the Soviet Union. A BBC magazine article that appeared November 10, 2008, stated:

> In Britain, many newspapers, notably Lord Beaverbrook's *Daily Express*, were hugely supportive of the Soviet war effort, and the fact that George Orwell could not get his brilliant satire on the Soviet state, *Animal Farm*, published during the war suggests that there was little appetite—to say the least—for balancing material about the horrors of life under Stalin.

This kid-glove treatment of the Soviet Union was not limited to Great Britain. In the United States, *Time* magazine named Joseph Stalin its Man of the Year for 1942, stating:

> The year 1942 was a year of blood and strength. The man whose name means steel in Russian, whose few words of English include the American expression "tough guy," was the man of 1942. Stalin's methods were tough, but they paid off.

Thus, the fortunes of war made a western hero out of a man who was responsible for the torture and death of millions of people.

In the selections that follow, commentators spanning more than sixty years examine Orwell's political beliefs and assess the political implications of *Animal Farm* as well as the role of politics in contemporary society. And although the world is no longer threatened by Soviet-style communism, Orwell's admonition about the tendency of power to corrupt remains relevant in the twenty-first century. As his biographer, George Woodcock, said in *The Crystal Spirit: A Study of George Orwell*:

Old and new tyrannies belong to the same family; authoritarian governments, whether they are based on the codes of old social castes or on the rules of new political elites, are basically similar and present similar dangers to human welfare and liberty.

Chronology

1903
George Orwell is born Eric Arthur Blair on June 25 in Motihari, Bengal, India, the second child and only son of Richard Walmesley Blair and Ida Mabel Limouzin Blair.

1904
Ida Blair returns to England with her two children and settles in Henley-on-Thames while her husband remains in India.

1908–11
Orwell attends Sunnylands, an Anglican school in Eastbourne, Sussex.

1911–16
Orwell attends St. Cyrian's preparatory school in Eastbourne as a boarder.

1912
Richard Blair retires from the India Civil Service and returns home. The family moves to Shiplake, Oxfordshire, near Henley.

1914
Orwell's first work—the poem "Awake Young Men of England"—is published.

1915
The Blair family returns to Henley-on-Thames.

1917–21
Narrowly missing a scholarship at Eton College, Orwell is accepted at Wellington College, where he spends the first nine weeks of 1917; however, a place opens for him at Eton College, and he transfers there in May as a King's Scholar. He graduates from Eton in 1921.

1921

The Blair family moves to Southwold, Suffolk.

1922–27

After passing an open examination, Orwell joins the Indian Imperial Police and serves as assistant superintendent of police in the force in Burma. His experiences cause him to develop a distaste for police work and to reject imperialism. He resigns while on leave in England in autumn of 1927, announces to his parents his intention to become a writer, and moves to the Notting Hill section of London.

1928–29

Determined to become a writer, Orwell lives in Paris for eighteen months. He develops pneumonia and is hospitalized for two weeks in spring of 1929 at Hôpital Cochin.

1930–31

Orwell returns to London and continues writing about social issues. He writes an early version of the autobiographical *Down and Out in Paris and London* and contributes "The Spike" and "The Hanging," two essays, to the journal *Adelphi* under his birth name.

1932–33

Orwell teaches at the Hawthorns, a small private school in Hayes, Middlesex.

1933

Orwell's first book, *Down and Out in Paris and London*, is published by Victor Gollancz. It relates Orwell's experiences among the working class and poor in Paris and London. Orwell teaches at Frays College, Uxbridge, Middlesex. In December, he is once more hospitalized with pneumonia.

1934

Orwell gives up teaching and spends ten months in South-wold. His first novel, *Burmese Days*, is published in the United States. He moves to Hampstead, London, in November and begins work in a bookshop. The bookshop is owned by members of the Independent Labour Party (ILP), a left-wing, socialist party that Orwell would join in 1938.

1935

A Clergyman's Daughter is published. *Burmese Days* is published in England. Orwell meets Eileen O'Shaughnessy.

1936

At the suggestion of publisher Victor Gollancz, Orwell investigates working-class life and unemployment in Lancashire and Yorkshire, which would result in the publication of *The Road to Wigan Pier* in 1937. Orwell and Eileen O'Shaughnessy marry in June. *Keep the Aspidistra Flying* is published. He attends ILP Summer School, Letchworth, Hertsfordshire. In December, he goes to Spain to cover the Spanish Civil War as a journalist, then joins a combat unit to fight fascism.

1937

Involved in street fighting in Barcelona, Orwell is wounded in the throat by a sniper. He receives an honorable discharge for medical reasons. *The Road to Wigan Pier* is published.

1938

Orwell suffers a tubercular hemorrhage in his lung and is hospitalized in a sanitarium in Kent for six months. *Homage to Catalonia* is published. He joins the ILP. With his wife, Orwell travels to Morocco for his health.

1939

Orwell returns to England. *Coming Up for Air* is published. Richard Blair dies. Orwell's opposition to the Hitler-Stalin Pact of August 1939 convinces him to support the war. He resigns from the pacifist ILP.

1940

Inside the Whale is published. Orwell moves to London and joins the Local Defense Volunteers (Home Guard). He writes reviews for *Time and Tide* and the *Tribune*.

1941

The Lion and the Unicorn is published. Orwell begins working for the British Broadcasting Corporation (BBC), preparing cultural talks for broadcast to Asia. He also writes reviews for the *Observer, Partisan Review*, and the *Manchester Evening News*.

1943

Ida Blair dies. Orwell becomes literary editor of the *Tribune*.

1944

The Orwells adopt a one-month-old baby boy, whom they name Richard Horatio Blair.

1945

Orwell serves as a war correspondent for the *Observer* in Paris and Cologne. Eileen dies while under anesthetic during a minor operation. *Animal Farm* is published.

1946

Critical Essays is published. Orwell moves to the Isle of Jura in the Inner Hebrides to live with his son and a nurse in an abandoned farmhouse, where he begins work on *Nineteen Eighty-Four*.

1947

Orwell is hospitalized again with tuberculosis in Hairmyres Hospital, near Glasgow, Scotland.

1948

Orwell returns to Jura in July and completes *Nineteen Eighty-Four*.

1949

Orwell enters Cotswolds Sanitorium in Cranham, Gloucestershire, and is then transferred to University College Hospital, London. *Nineteen Eighty-Four* is published in June and more than four hundred thousand copies are sold the first year. While in the hospital in October, he marries Sonia Bronwell, an editorial assistant with *Horizon*.

1950

Orwell dies suddenly in University College Hospital from a fatal pulmonary hemorrhage on January 21. He is buried at the Church of All Saints, Sutton Courtenay, Oxfordshire.

Social Issues
in Literature

CHAPTER 1

Background on George Orwell

The Life of George Orwell

Contemporary Authors

The Contemporary Authors *database is published online by Gale, a part of Cengage Learning.*

George Orwell's personal experiences—including his unhappy time at an English preparatory school, his duty as a policeman in Burma, and his service in the Spanish Civil War—shaped his political views and his writing, according to the editors of the following article. A political writer, Orwell in his best books expressed his concerns with social welfare, individualism, and truth. He was a man with a generous spirit who distrusted rigid ideologies and had a strong belief in the value of common sense and human decency.

"Liberty," wrote Eric Blair under his famous pseudonym of George Orwell, "is telling people what they do not want to hear." Orwell is best known for his novels *Animal Farm* and *Nineteen Eighty-Four*, which warn that the growing power of modern governments—regardless of their ideology—threatens to obliterate such widely held ideals as love of family, tolerance towards others, and the right to make up one's own mind. Convinced that human decency and common sense were the basis of a just society, the author repeatedly found himself in conflict with the ideological mass movements of his time, ranging from capitalism to fascism and communism. Orwell, wrote Laurence Brander, "was an individualist" who confronted "contemporary social and political problems . . . as a man who has done all his thinking for himself." Mistrusting the broad theories of twentieth-century political thinkers, he remained faithful to the truth of his own experience. "These qualities are rare and valuable," Brander declared, "and they are natural sources of his popularity with readers who must learn, like him, to work things out for themselves."

Experience Shaped Orwell's Writing

Orwell never wrote an autobiography and in personal conversations he was notably reserved. But as a writer who shunned abstract theory in favor of concrete detail, he gravitated toward the subject matter he knew best: his own life and thoughts. As George Woodcock cautioned, however, "the autobiographical form of [Orwell's] works can be deceptive, if it is taken too literally." At heart, Woodcock suggested, Orwell was a moralist, deeply concerned with the proper conduct of human life. His personal experiences raised ethical questions that he shared with his readers.

"From a very early age . . . I knew that when I grew up I should be a writer," said Orwell in his 1946 essay "Why I Write." Interestingly, Orwell claimed that he first saw writing as a remedy for loneliness. Born in colonial India to a low-level British official, he was sent to England as an infant along with his mother. He was eight and ready for boarding school by the time his father rejoined the family permanently. On the whole Orwell's family seems to have been fairly undemonstrative; his later adulation of family life, Woodcock suggested, may have sprung from feeling emotionally deprived during his youth. If Orwell's family disappointed him, his small hometown of Henley-on-Thames brought compensations. From there he explored the English countryside, fishing, hiking, and learning about animals. Later Orwell appeared to view Henley and its surroundings as symbolic of a calmer, saner world that existed in England before the two world wars. "By retaining one's childhood love of such things as trees, fishes, butterflies, and . . . [even] toads," he wrote, "one makes a peaceful world a little more probable," for if the world is only "steel and concrete . . . human beings will have no outlet for their surplus energy except in hatred and leader worship."

Boarding school was a source of lasting bitterness for Orwell—particularly the English preparatory school, where preteenage children were rigorously prepared to enter elite secondary schools and prestigious careers. His experience at St. Cyprian's prep school appears in "Such, Such Were the Joys," an article that Cyril Connolly called the "key to his formation." Judged by this study, St. Cyprian's provided some of Orwell's first glimpses into the misuse of power and the unfairness of England's class-conscious society. "I was in a world where it was *not possible* for me to be good," he wrote of the school's capricious discipline. As a scholarship student, he found that his background in the "lower-upper-middle class"—pursuing upper-class values on a middle-class income—invited the contempt of both his headmaster and his wealthy peers. "In a world where the prime necessities were money, titled relatives, athleticism, tailor-made clothes, neatly-brushed hair, a charming smile, I was no good," the author wrote. "[I knew] that the future was dark. Failure, failure, failure—failure behind me, failure ahead of me—that was by far the deepest conviction that I carried away." Hailed as the most unsparing account of English private schools ever written, "Such, Such Were the Joys" also shows the problem of interpreting Orwell's autobiographical work. Orwell never published this essay and when it appeared after his death, admirers of St. Cyprian's declared it inaccurate. Less partisan observers—including biographer Bernard Crick—note that the author's grim tone, and the insights he claims to have gained as a child, seem too broadly stated to be completely credible. After investigating Orwell's accusations, Crick concluded that while some details had been exaggerated for rhetorical effect, "the school seems to have been a pretty despicable place." Orwell's plight, Crick declared, "was an agony that he never forgot, but he put it to good use to understand the psychology of the poor and oppressed in his early writings and, later on, to champion their causes."

Ironically Orwell was a success by St. Cyprian's standards, going on to Eton College, England's most prestigious secondary school. In its tolerant atmosphere he became rebellious, shunning class work and team sports in favor of reading or swimming on his own. After graduating in 1921 he had no prospect of entering a major university and showed few regrets. On an apparent whim he volunteered to become a policeman in the Burma branch of the Indian Imperial Police. Five years later he returned to England on medical leave, possibly suffering an early bout of tuberculosis. To the consternation of superiors, he quit without giving an explanation; to the dismay of his parents, he announced he would become a writer, a career in which he had little training or experience. Clearly Burma disturbed Orwell profoundly, although his reticence has kept biographers from knowing many of the personal details. In some of his most admired early writings, however, he alluded to those years with shame and indignation. As he explained in *The Road to Wigan Pier,* "In order to hate imperialism you have got to be part of it." One of Orwell's earliest works is the 1931 essay "A Hanging," which Crick called "the first piece of writing that shows [his] distinctive style and powers." In an observant, plain-spoken, subtly paced narrative the author recalled an execution in the courtyard of a Burmese prison. The condemned man's smallest act—stepping to avoid a puddle—brings Orwell an unsettling awareness that execution means destroying a living consciousness. Once the man is dead, Orwell seems relieved to join the other witnesses in empty-headed chatter. . . .

Most Successful Works Are Political

The constricted life of the white conqueror informs Orwell's first published novel, *Burmese Days* (1934). The main character is John Flory, administrator for a British lumber company in Burma. Flory's skeptical view of colonialism parallels

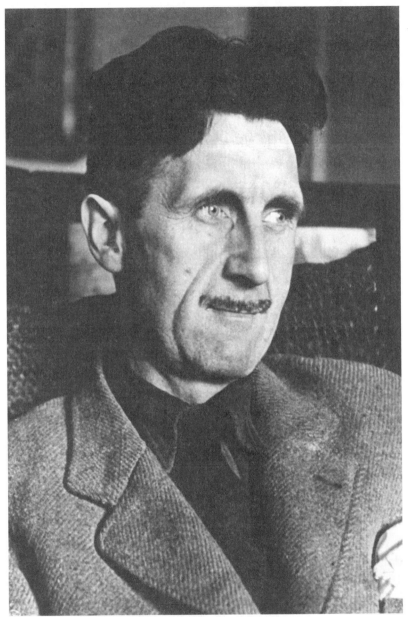

George Orwell (pseudonym of Eric Arthur Blair). Popperfoto/Getty Images.

Orwell's own, but at age thirty-five, Flory seems more bitter than Orwell was when he quit Burma in his mid-twenties. As biographer Averil Gardner suggested, Flory can be seen as a portrait of the desperately isolated man Orwell feared he would become if he had stayed. . . .

Upon returning from Burma, Orwell recalled in *The Road to Wigan Pier*, "I was conscious of an immense weight of guilt that I had got to expiate. I suppose that sounds exaggerated; but if you do for five years a job that you thoroughly disapprove of, you will probably feel the same." He described himself to colleagues as a "Tory anarchist," which seems to mean that he respected traditional ethics but mistrusted any authority that might enforce them. "I now realised that there was no need to go as far as Burma to find tyranny and exploitation," Orwell continued, because the lower classes of Europe were oppressed by poverty just as the Burmese were oppressed by British arms. Unfamiliar with the everyday struggles of the working poor, Orwell was drawn to the more blatant deprivation of tramps and beggars. As writer Jack London had done years before, he dressed as a tramp and explored the London underworld of flophouses and soup kitchens. He also spent nearly two years as a struggling writer in Paris, ending up a penniless dishwasher. These experiences inspired his first published book, *Down and Out in Paris and London* (1933). Autobiographical in form, it is basically a work of social reportage: "Poverty," Orwell declared, "is what I am writing about." At its best *Down and Out* resembles "A Hanging" by mixing social concern with acute observations on human nature. . . .

Orwell's third and fourth books, both novels, reflect his demoralizing struggle to establish himself as a writer. As the 1930s began he had just returned from Paris, having written a series of novels and short stories that he destroyed when they proved unpublishable. His Paris adventure, not yet a book, seemed a fiasco; his savings from Burma were exhausted; and the Great Depression was deepening. For several years he worked reluctantly as a private-school teacher and a bookstore clerk, taking solace in the Anglican religion of his childhood.

A Clergyman's Daughter and *Keep the Aspidistra Flying* seem to be fictionalized accounts of his frustrations. In each novel, as in *Burmese Days*, an isolated individual tries and fails to transcend his or her social role. . . . Orwell considered these his weakest books, and his admirers generally respect his judgment. Both novels are marred by mechanistic plots: the clergyman's daughter, complained *New Statesman's* Peter Quennell, is "a literary abstraction to whom things happen." Similarly, [*Keep the Aspidistra Flying's* Gordon] Comstock is so dominated by bitterness that his interactions with others seem unconvincing.

"Looking back through my work," Orwell later observed, "I see that it is invariably where I lacked a *political* purpose that I wrote lifeless books." Orwell's writing gained new effectiveness when he found a political focus for his discontent. The high ideals of socialism—economic justice in a democratic society—became a standard by which he judged the world around him. In the mid-1930s, socialist publisher Victor Gollancz commissioned Orwell to write a book on the industrial workers of northern England. There the author gained his first personal contact with the working class—not the outcasts he met as a tramp, but a large segment of society in which hard labor and poverty consumed whole families. His outraged report on the plight of English workers in *The Road to Wigan Pier* displayed his skill as a writer and his new political consciousness. . . . "There was such an extraordinary change both in his writing and . . . in his attitude after he'd been to the North and written that book," said magazine publisher Richard Rees. "It was almost as if there'd been a kind of fire smouldering in him all his life which suddenly broke into flame." In the second half of *Wigan Pier*—included against Gollancz's wishes—Orwell defined his personal commitment to socialism. Analyzing his background, he denounced his work in Burma and the middle-class snobbery he learned in childhood. Then, in a notoriously opinionated fashion, he reviewed English socialism with equal frankness. His basic ideas were arguably sound: socialist leaders, fixed on Marxist theories such as class conflict, risked losing the public by seeming narrow-minded and intolerant; to fight the rise of fascism, they should unite the lower and middle classes in a broad crusade for liberty and justice. But as [critic Walter] Greenwood noted, the author "has you with him one moment and provoked beyond endurance the next." Socialism, Orwell continued, repelled working people because of its intellectual "cranks," including feminists and advocates of birth control: workers who avoided higher education had more common sense. Such notions were sure to appall many patrons of Gollancz's Left Book Club, and the publisher added an introduction to *Wigan Pier* that chided the author for narrow-mindedness.

The Spanish Civil War

Orwell appeared untroubled by the controversy. After years of seeming too poor, homely, or eccentric to attract a wife, he married Eileen O'Shaughnessy and settled happily into life as a village grocer with farm animals in his backyard. He was greatly disturbed, however, by the outbreak of civil war in Spain, where the democratically elected government was menaced by an invading army of fascist rebels. By 1937 he and Eileen were in the Spanish province of Catalonia, where he joined an antifascist militia organized by the Workers' Party of Marxist Unity (POUM) and she worked behind the lines. The couple was drawn into a heartbreaking conflict between personal ideals and power politics, chronicled by Orwell in *Homage to Catalonia*. As the author quickly realized, Spanish leftists had answered the fascist invasion by starting their own revolution behind government lines. . . .

Soon POUM and other prominent supporters of the Catalonian workers' revolt were suppressed by government police. It has been argued that the government acted from military necessity, but Orwell was appalled to see the Spanish Communists aiding the suppression. He surmised with good reason that they and their Soviet advisers had abandoned the idealistic leftists in a bid to increase their own power. As a writer Orwell was outraged by the ability of Communists to spread lies about POUM, including the widely accepted claim that the group was secretly allied to fascism. He watched helplessly as POUM militiamen, returning from the front lines, were arrested in Barcelona and imprisoned. Recovering from a shot to the throat that he received while on duty, Orwell was lucky to find his wife and escape from Spain alive. As its title suggests, *Homage to Catalonia* was his tribute to the colleagues he left behind. The book was coolly received when it first appeared, for its praise of socialist ideals made it of interest primarily to the Left, yet it criticized leftists for fratricide and susceptibility to propaganda. . . .

Homage to Catalonia marked the emergence of Orwell's mature writing style, which used simple but eloquent prose to convey his concerns for social welfare, individuality, and honesty. "Good prose," he said in "Why I Write," "is like a windowpane." He soon gained a wide audience for his expository writing, which ranged from columns and book reviews to formal essays. Though his articles sometimes display the name-calling that irked readers of *Wigan Pier*, overall they have been lauded for originality, candor, and open-mindedness. . . .

For Orwell and many others, the Spanish Civil War presaged a broader conflict with fascism that would embroil all Europe. He increasingly dreaded the consequences of such a war concerned that in the name of military necessity many humane ideals—especially the socialist hope of liberty with economic justice—would disappear even without a fascist victory. He advocated pacifism and published a fourth novel, *Coming Up for Air*, that contrasted the menacing world around him with the peace he had known as a child. The book centers on George Bowling, a London salesman plagued by workaday frustrations and by the sense that both fascists and their opponents are filling the world with obsessive hate. During a nostalgic escape to his small hometown, he finds that while his childhood memories are vivid and warm, the town has become ugly and industrialized. Finally he returns home, resolved to face the world's problems as best he can. A few months after the book was published in 1939, World War II began and Orwell swung from pacifism to patriotism. Because of his tuberculosis and his service in the POUM militia, his attempts to join the war effort were often rebuffed, but eventually he entered the civil defense forces and produced radio programs for the British Broadcasting Corporation (BBC). . . . Orwell's work at the BBC, however, revived his fears about a national mobilization. While preparing cultural talks for broadcast to Asia, he found himself repeatedly compelled to avoid such pressing issues as Asian self-rule and the fate of colonialism. Pleading ill health, he resigned his post and began work on two new novels.

Finding Artistic and Commercial Success

Orwell revived a project that may date back to his time in Spain, in which he hoped to explain his fears for society through a simple story. In particular, at a time when Soviet dictator Joseph Stalin was widely praised for battling Nazi Germany, he wished to separate socialist ideals from Stalin's self-serving distortions of them. "One day," Orwell later recalled, "I saw a little boy . . . driving a huge cart-horse along a narrow path, whipping it whenever it tried to turn. It struck me that if only such animals became aware of their strength we should have no power over them, and that men exploit animals in much the same way as the rich exploit the proletariat." His fantasy became *Animal Farm*, the tale of a barnyard revolt against human masters that parallels the rise and decline of socialism in the Soviet Union. The story opens as animals expel Mr. Jones from his farm and create an "animalist" republic. Most animals have simple dreams of justice, but the pigs are greedy and cunning, and in the end they use "animalist" rhetoric to justify their own tyranny. *Animal Farm* is considered an amazingly successful blend of political satire and childlike fable: Orwell was both a student of Soviet politics and a lover of animals. Completed in 1944, the book remained unpublished for more than a year because British firms, sometimes on government advice, declined to offend the country's Soviet allies. When the small leftist firm of Secker & Warburg printed it, publisher and author suddenly became affluent.

Meanwhile, horrified by government suppression of pacifists (whom he had denounced during his wartime fervor), Orwell became vice-chair of a civil liberties organization called the Freedom Defence Committee. To show that the wrongs of the Soviet state might occur in any society, he set his next novel in the England of the near future and eventually titled it *Nineteen Eighty-Four*. The book is so grim that some literary critics, noting Orwell's declining health, have surmised that it shows the collapse of his spirit. Arguably, however, it is a summation of themes and ideas from throughout his life and work. In *Nineteen Eighty-Four* the world is divided among three warring superstates, and England is essentially a colony of America—whose people Orwell often accused of enjoying casual brutality. The main character is Winston Smith, who works in London for the Ministry of Truth. In a caricature of Orwell's BBC work and of Spanish Communist propaganda, Winston spends his day rewriting history, employing bits of a new language—Newspeak—designed to make unpatriotic thoughts impossible to express. . . . Like typical Orwell characters, Winston makes a doomed effort to free himself. . . . Soon Winston and his lover are imprisoned and brainwashed, reduced to a childish helplessness Orwell may have made more graphic by recalling his days at St. Cyprian's. Winston's torturer coolly admits the Party's ethic of power for its own sake, depicting the future as "a boot stamping on a human face— for ever."

The very success of *Nineteen Eighty-Four* and *Animal Farm* brought Orwell new troubles, as a new generation of readers—particularly Americans—failed to note his longstanding interest in humane socialism and praised him as a conservative anticommunist. He heightened the impression by using the word "Ingsoc," suggesting a debased English socialism, as the name of the state ideology in *Nineteen Eighty-Four*. Increasingly ill with tuberculosis, Orwell met in his hospital with publisher Fred Warburg and helped compose a press release, which noted that "in the U.S.A. the phrase . . . 'hundred percent Americanism' is suitable and the qualifying adjective is as totalitarian as anyone could wish." The book, they averred, was a warning, not a fatalistic prediction, and they summarized its moral as "*Don't let it happen. It depends on you.*" Meanwhile Orwell faced personal crises. He downplayed his illness, seemingly determined to retain an active life. After Eileen died in 1945 he responded by working harder. Left to care for the couple's adopted son, he appears to have been far more interested than most fathers of his time in the child's welfare. The limited drug therapy available for tuberculosis proved torturous and futile, and in 1950—a few months after his second marriage—he died at the age of forty-six.

A Posthumous Legend

Orwell's long struggle for success, his willingness to brave controversy, and his untimely death helped make him a figure of legend. In a famous obituary for *New Statesman*, V.S. Pritchett called him "the wintry conscience of a generation" and "a kind of saint." Soon such accolades were broadened by less discerning observers into a general veneration of Orwell's writings and actions, prompting even well-known admirers such as Woodcock to allude to an "Orwell Industry" or "Cult."

Both liberals and conservatives claimed to be his political heirs, while skeptics called him overrated or irrelevant to a changing world. As Orwell himself observed, "saints should always be judged guilty until they are proved innocent." Skeptics justifiably recall that Orwell could be aloof and opinionated as well as warmhearted and tolerant. He never created a consistent system of philosophy, and even seemed to relish human inconsistencies as a force for social moderation. His strengths, accordingly, are difficult to summarize. He may have done the best job himself when he described Charles Dickens, an author whose social concern and faith in human decency he greatly admired. As Crick and others have suggested, the virtues Orwell saw in Dickens were the ones he probably valued in himself. "I see . . . a man who is always fighting against something," Orwell wrote, "but who fights in the open and is not frightened . . . a man who is *generously angry*—in other words . . . a nineteenth-century liberal, a free intelligence, a type hated with equal hatred by all the smelly little orthodoxies which are now contending for our souls." As long as there are orthodoxies, there will be a need for Orwell.

Intellectual Censorship Made Publishing *Animal Farm* Difficult

George Orwell

George Orwell was a major twentieth-century novelist, essayist, and short-story writer. His best-known works are Animal Farm *and* Nineteen Eighty-Four.

Animal Farm was a highly controversial book for its time because it was critical of the USSR during World War II, when the USSR was an ally of Orwell's country, Great Britain, against Nazi Germany. The novel was turned down by four publishers before Orwell finally found one willing to publish it. The following selection is the preface that he intended for his novel. Because of its challenging nature, this preface was not included in the novel and was only discovered among Orwell's papers some years after the novel's publication. In this piece, Orwell writes of the censorship that can occur in a democracy when the press is unwilling to support an unpopular position.

[A*nimal Farm]* was first thought of, so far as the central idea goes, in 1937, but was not written down until about the end of 1943. By the time when it came to be written it was obvious that there would be great difficulty in getting it published (in spite of the present book shortage which ensures that anything describable as a book will "sell"), and in the event it was refused by four publishers. Only one of these had any ideological motive. Two had been publishing anti-Russian books for years, and the other had no noticeable political   colour. One publisher actually started by accepting the book, but

George Orwell, "The Freedom of the Press," *New Statesman & Society*, vol. 8, no. 366, August 18, 1995, pp. 11–15. Copyright © 1995 New Statesman, Ltd. Reproduced by permission.

after making the preliminary arrangements he decided to consult the Ministry of Information, who appear to have warned him, or at any rate strongly advised him, against publishing it. Here is an extract from his letter:

> I mentioned the reaction I had had from an important official in the Ministry of Information [MOI] with regard to *Animal Farm*. I must confess that this expression of opinion has given me seriously to think. I can see now that it might be regarded as something which it was highly ill-advised to publish at the present time. If the fable were addressed generally to dictators and dictatorships at large then publication would be all right, but the fable does follow, as I see now, so completely the progress of the Russian Soviets and their two dictators, that it can apply only to Russia, to the exclusion of the other dictatorships. Another thing: it would be less offensive if the predominant caste in the fable were not pigs. I think the choice of pigs as the ruling caste will no doubt give offence to many people, and particularly to anyone who is a bit touchy, as undoubtedly the Russians are.

The Worst Type of Censorship

This kind of thing is not a good symptom. Obviously it is not desirable that a government department should have any power of censorship (except security censorship, which no one objects to in war time) over books which are not officially sponsored. But the chief danger to freedom of thought and speech at this moment is not the direct interference of the MOI or any official body.

If publishers and editors exert themselves to keep certain topics out of print, it is not because they are frightened of prosecution but because they are frightened of public opinion. In [Great Britain] intellectual cowardice is the worst enemy a writer or journalist has to face, and that fact does not seem to me to have had the discussion it deserves.

Any fairminded person with journalistic experience will admit that during this war official censorship has not been particularly irksome. We have not been subjected to the kind of totalitarian "co-ordination" that it might have been reasonable to expect. The press has some justified grievances, but on the whole the government has behaved well and has been surprisingly tolerant of minority opinions. The sinister fact about literary censorship in England is that it is largely voluntary. Unpopular ideas can be silenced, and inconvenient facts kept dark, without the need for any official ban.

Anyone who has lived long in a foreign country will know of instances of sensational items of news things which on their own merits would get the big headlines—being kept right out of the British press, not because the government intervened but because of a general tacit agreement that "it wouldn't do" to mention that particular fact. So far as the daily newspapers go, this is easy to understand. The British press is extremely centralised, and most of it is owned by wealthy men who have every motive to be dishonest on certain important topics. But the same kind of veiled censorship also operates in books and periodicals, as well as in plays, films and radio. At any given moment there is an orthodoxy, a body of ideas which it is assumed that all right-thinking people will accept without question.

It is not exactly forbidden to say this, that or the other, but it is "not done" to say it, just as in mid-Victorian times it was "not done" to mention trousers in the presence of a lady. Anyone who challenges the prevailing orthodoxy finds himself silenced with surprising effectiveness. A genuinely unfashionable opinion is almost never given a fair hearing, either in the popular press or in the highbrow periodicals.

Politically Incorrect to Criticize Soviets

At this moment what is demanded by the prevailing orthodoxy is an uncritical admiration of Soviet Russia. Everyone knows this, nearly everyone acts on it. Any serious criticism of the Soviet regime, any disclosure of facts which the Soviet government would prefer to keep hidden, is next door to unprintable. And this nation-wide conspiracy to flatter our ally takes place, curiously enough, against a background of genuine intellectual tolerance. For though you are not allowed to criticise the Soviet government, at least you are reasonably free to criticise our own. Hardly anyone will print an attack on [Joseph] Stalin, but it is quite safe to attack [Winston] Churchill, at any rate in books and periodicals. And throughout five years of war, during two or three of which we were fighting for national survival, countless books, pamphlets and articles advocating a compromise peace have been published without interference. More, they have been published without exciting much disapproval.

So long as the prestige of the USSR is not involved, the principle of free speech has been reasonably well upheld. There are other forbidden topics . . . , but the prevailing attitude towards the USSR is much the most serious symptom. It is, as it were, spontaneous, and is not due to the action of any pressure group.

The servility with which the greater part of the English intelligentsia have swallowed and repeated Russian propaganda from 1941 onwards would be quite astounding if it were not that they have behaved similarly on several earlier occasions. On one controversial issue after another the Russian viewpoint has been accepted without examination and then publicised with complete disregard to historical truth or intellectual decency.

To name only one instance, the BBC celebrated the 25th anniversary of the Red Army without mentioning [Leon] Trotsky. This was about as accurate as commemorating the battle of Trafalgar without mentioning [Horatio] Nelson, but it evoked no protest from the English intelligentsia. In the internal struggles in the various occupied countries, the British press has in almost all cases sided with the faction favoured by the Russians and libelled the opposing faction, sometimes suppressing material evidence in order to do so. A particularly glaring case was that of Colonel [Draja] Mihailovich, the Jugoslav Chetnik leader. The Russians, who had their own Jugoslav protege in Marshal [Josip] Tito, accused Mihailovich of collaborating with the Germans. This accusation was promptly taken up by the British press: Mihailovich's supporters were given no chance of answering it, and facts contradicting it were simply kept out of print.

In July of 1943, the Germans offered a reward of 100,000 gold crowns for the capture of Tito, and a similar reward for the capture of Mihailovich. The British press "splashed" the reward for Tito, but only one paper mentioned (in small print) the reward for Mihailovich: and the charges of collaborating with the Germans continued.

Very similar things happened during the Spanish civil war. Then, too, the factions on the Republican side which the Russians were determined to crush were recklessly libelled in the English left-wing press, and any statement in their defence even in letter form, was refused publication. At present, not only is serious criticism of the USSR considered reprehensible, but even the fact of the existence of such criticism is kept secret in some cases. For example, shortly before his death Trotsky had written a biography of Stalin. One may assume that it was not an altogether unbiased book, but obviously it was saleable.

An American publisher had arranged to issue it and the book was in print—I believe the review copies had been sent out—when the USSR entered the war. The book was immediately withdrawn. Not a word about this has ever appeared in the British press, though clearly the existence of such a book, and its suppression, was a news item worth a few paragraphs.

Several Kinds of Censorship in England

It is important to distinguish between the kind of censorship that the English literary intelligentsia voluntarily impose upon themselves, and the censorship that can sometimes be enforced by pressure groups. Notoriously, certain topics cannot be discussed because of "vested interests". The best-known case is the patent medicine racket. Again, the Catholic Church has considerable influence in the press and can silence criticism of itself to some extent. . . .

But this kind of thing is harmless, or at least it is understandable. Any large organisation will look after its own interests as best it can, and overt propaganda is not a thing to object to. One would no more expect the *Daily Worker* to publicise unfavourable facts about the USSR than one would expect the *Catholic Herald* to denounce the Pope. But then every thinking person knows the *Daily Worker* and the *Catholic Herald* for what they are. What is disquieting is that where the USSR and its policies are concerned one cannot expect intelligent criticism or even, in many cases, plain honesty from Liberal writers and journalists who are under no direct pressure to falsify their opinions. Stalin is sacrosanct and certain aspects of his policy must not be seriously discussed. This rule has been almost universally observed since 1941, but it had operated, to a greater extent than is sometimes realised, for ten years earlier than that. Throughout that time, criticism of the Soviet regime from the left could only obtain a hearing with difficulty.

There was a huge output of anti-Russian literature, but nearly all of it was from the Conservative angle and manifestly dishonest, out of date and actuated by sordid motives. On the other side there was an equally huge and almost equally dishonest stream of pro-Russian propaganda, and what amounted to a boycott on anyone who tried to discuss all-important questions in a grown-up manner. You could, indeed, publish anti-Russian books, but to do so was to make sure of being ignored or misrepresented by nearly the whole of the highbrow press. Both publicly and privately you were warned that it was "not done". What you said might possibly be true, but it was "inopportune" and "played into the hands of" this or that reactionary interest.

This attitude was usually defended on the ground that the international situation, and the urgent need for an Anglo-Russian alliance, demanded it; but it was clear that this was a rationalisation. The English intelligentsia, or a great part of it, had developed a nationalistic loyalty towards the USSR, and in their hearts they felt that to cast any doubt on the wisdom of Stalin was a kind of blasphemy. Events in Russia and events elsewhere were to be judged by different standards. The endless executions in the purges of 1936–38 were applauded by life-long opponents of capital punishment, and it was considered equally proper to publicise famines when they happened in India and to conceal them when they happened in the Ukraine. And if this was true before the war, the intellectual atmosphere is certainly no better now.

Intelligentsia Harm Freedom of Speech

But now to come back to this book of mine. The reaction towards it of most English intellectuals will be quite simple: "It oughtn't to have been published." Naturally, those reviewers who understand the art of denigration will not attack it on political grounds but on literary ones. They will say that it is a dull, silly book and a disgraceful waste of paper. This may well be true, but it is obviously not the whole of the story. One does not say that a book "ought not to have been published" merely because it is a bad book. After all, acres of rubbish are presented daily and no one bothers.

The English intelligentsia, or most of them, will object to this book because it traduces their Leader and (as they see it) does harm to the cause of progress. If it did the opposite they would have nothing to say against it, even if its literary faults were ten times as glaring as they are. The success of, for instance, the Left Book Club over a period of four or five years shows how willing they are to tolerate both scurrility and slip-shod writing, provided it tells them what they want to hear.

The issue involved here is quite a simple one: is every opinion, however unpopular—however foolish, even—entitled to a hearing? Put it in that form and nearly any English intellectual will feel that he ought to say "Yes". But give it a concrete shape, and ask, "How about an attack on Stalin? Is that entitled to a hearing?", and the answer more often than not will be "No". In that case the current orthodoxy happens to be challenged, and so the principle of free speech lapses.

Now, when one demands liberty of speech and of the press, one is not demanding absolute liberty. There always must be, or at any rate there always will be, some degree of censorship, so long as organised societies endure. But freedom, as [left-wing revolutionary political writer] Rosa Luxemburg said, is "freedom for the other fellow". The same principle is contained in the famous words of Voltaire: "I detest what you say; I will defend to the death your right to say it." If the intellectual liberty which without a doubt has been one of the distinguishing marks of western civilisation means anything at all, it means that everyone shall have the right to say and to print what he believes to be the truth, provided only that it does not harm the rest of the community in some quite unmistakable way. Both capitalist democracy and the western versions of Socialism have till recently taken that principle for granted. Our government, as I have already pointed out, still makes some show of respecting it. The ordinary people in the street—partly, perhaps, because they are not sufficiently interested in ideas to be intolerant about them—still vaguely hold that "I suppose everyone's got a right to their own opinion". It is only, or at any rate it is chiefly, the literary and scientific intelligentsia, the very people who ought to be the guardians of liberty, who are beginning to despise it, in theory as well as in practice.

One of the peculiar phenomena of our time is the renegade Liberal. Over and above the familiar Marxist claim that "bourgeois liberty" is an illusion, there is now a widespread tendency to argue that one can only defend democracy by totalitarian methods. If one loves democracy, the argument runs, one must crush its enemies by no matter what means. And who are its enemies? It always appears that they are not only those who attack it openly and consciously, but those who "objectively" endanger it by spreading mistaken doctrines. In other words, defending democracy involves destroying all independence of thought. This argument was used, for instance, to justify the Russian purges. The most ardent Russophile hardly believed that all of the victims were guilty of all the things they were accused of: but by holding heretical opinions they "objectively" harmed the regime, and therefore it was quite right not only to massacre them but to discredit them by false accusations. The same argument was used to justify the quite conscious lying that went on in the left-wing press about the Trotskyists and other Republican minorities in the Spanish civil war. . . . These people don't see that if you encourage totalitarian methods, the time may come when they will be used against you instead of for you. Make a habit of imprisoning Fascists without trial, and perhaps the process won't stop at Fascists.

Soon after the suppressed *Daily Worker* had been reinstated, I was lecturing to a workingmen's college in South London. The audience were working-class and lower-middle class intellectuals—the same sort of audience that one used to meet at Left Book Club branches. The lecture had touched on the freedom of the press, and at the end, to my astonishment, several questioners stood up and asked me: Did I not think that the lifting of the ban on the *Daily Worker* was a great mistake? When asked why, they said that it was a paper of doubtful loyalty and ought not to be tolerated in war time. I found myself defending the *Daily Worker*, which has gone out of its way to libel me more than once.

But where had these people learned this essentially totalitarian outlook? Pretty certainly they had learned it from the Communists themselves! Tolerance and decency are deeply rooted in England, but they are not indestructible, and they have to be kept alive partly by conscious effort. The result of preaching totalitarian doctrines is to weaken the instinct by means of which free peoples know what is or is not dangerous. . . .

I am well acquainted with all the arguments against freedom of thought and speech—the arguments which claim that it cannot exist, and the arguments which claim that it ought not to. I answer simply that they don't convince me and that our civilisation over a period of 400 years has been founded on the opposite notice. For quite a decade past I have believed that the existing Russian regime is a mainly evil thing, and I claim the right to say so, in spite of the fact that we are allies with the USSR in a war which I want to see won. If I had to choose a text to justify myself, I should choose the line from [John] Milton:

"By the known rules of ancient liberty."

Political Expediency over Free Speech

The word ancient emphasises the fact that intellectual freedom is a deep-rooted tradition without which our characteristic western culture could only doubtfully exist. From that tradition many of our intellectuals are visibly turning away. They have accepted the principle that a book should be published or suppressed, praised or damned, not on its merits but according to political expediency. And others who do not actually hold this view assent to it from sheer cowardice.

An example of this is the failure of the numerous and vocal English pacifists to raise their voices against the prevalent worship of Russian militarism. According to those pacifists, all violence is evil, and they have urged us at every stage of the war to give in or at least to make a compromise peace. But how many of them have ever suggested that war is also evil when it is waged by the Red Army? Apparently the Russians have a right to defend themselves, whereas for us to do so is a deadly sin.

One can only explain this contradiction in one way: that is, by a cowardly desire to keep in with the bulk of the intelligentsia, whose patriotism is directed towards the USSR rather than towards Britain. I know that the English intelligentsia have plenty of reason for their timidity and dishonesty, indeed I know by heart the arguments by which they justify themselves. But at least let us have no more nonsense about defending liberty against Fascism.

If liberty means anything at all it means the right to tell people what they do not want to hear. The common people still vaguely subscribe to that doctrine and act on it. In our country—it is not the same in all countries: it was not so in republican France, and it is not so in the USA today—it is the liberals who fear liberty and the intellectuals who want to do dirt on the intellect: it is to draw attention to that fact that I have written this preface.

Orwell Remains Relevant in the Twenty-First Century

John P. Rossi

John P. Rossi is professor emeritus of history at La Salle University in Philadelphia.

Despite the fact that the political systems Orwell warned against in his writings are no longer a threat, his work remains relevant, according to John P. Rossi in the following essay. Orwell was not only preaching against the evils of communism, fascism, and imperialism; Rossi points out that he was also warning about the way language can be corrupted to disguise the truth. Although Orwell was a socialist, Rossi explains, his concern about the control of too much power by a central government has caused him to be embraced by the right as well as the left.

This year [2003] marks the centenary of the birth of Eric Arthur Blair, better known as George Orwell. Although dead for over a half century, Orwell remains one of the most read and most quoted authors of the twentieth century. His two best-known books, *Animal Farm* and *Nineteen Eighty-Four*, remain in print and have sold over 30 million copies. They contributed such phrases to the language as 'Big Brother', 'Newspeak', 'All animals are equal but some are more equal than others'. In 1996 a poll of its customers by the English bookstore, Waterstone's, ranked *Animal Farm* and *Nineteen Eighty-Four* as the second and third most influential books of the twentieth century, trailing only J.R.R. Tolkien's *Lord of the Rings*.

Biographies and special studies about Orwell still appear with regularity: a life by the biographer Jeffrey Meyers was

John P. Rossi, "The Enduring Relevance of George Orwell," *Contemporary Review*, vol. 283, no. 1652, September 1, 2003, pp. 172–176. Reproduced by the permission of Contemporary Review Ltd.

published in 2000, several biographies and studies have appeared in this centenary year, including one by the controversial journalist Christopher Hitchens who stresses Orwell's continuing importance today. Only last month [August 2003] two prominent Democratic politicians in America, Senator [Joseph] Lieberman and former Vice-President [Al] Gore used some of Orwell's words to attack President [George W.] Bush.

Appeal for Both Left and Right

Why does this writer continue to fascinate critics and ordinary readers today? Why Orwell's enduring relevance?

Orwell, quite simply, continues to fascinate as a writer and a person. His literary output includes a brace of still readable novels, two works of pure genius (the aforementioned *Animal Farm* and *Nineteen Eighty-Four*) along with some of the best essays to appear in the first half of the twentieth century.

Orwell's political writings, especially his exposure of Communism, Fascism and Imperialism, may seem dated now when these isms—at least in the form Orwell knew them—are dead. But a closer look reveals the sophistication of Orwell's insights. He was concerned not only about the disastrous effect of totalitarianism but also about the way it corrupted the language and thus made seeking the truth more difficult. He feared the growing power of the centralized state, seeing in it a threat to individual liberty. For these reasons Orwell's appeal crosses the political spectrum. The right has tried to co-opt him: 'body snatching', Hitchens calls it, claiming Orwell as the first Cold Warrior. In fact, there is some evidence that he coined the term 'Cold War' as early as October 1945. For his fellow leftists, he is the champion of egalitarianism and foe of privilege, a prime example of Socialism with a human face.

Not an Early Success

Orwell's early years were typical of the respectable middle classes (he was always precise about his status, labelling himself lower upper middle class) in Edwardian England. He attended St. Cyprians, a decent preparatory school, and then won a scholarship to one of the leading public schools, Eton. He failed to distinguish himself; and, instead of taking the traditional route to Oxford or Cambridge, Orwell followed in his father's path into the Indian Imperial Police, serving in Burma. He spent an unusual five-year apprenticeship there absorbing a hatred of British imperialism, a distrust of authority and a growing desire to rid himself of an attitude of superiority to the native populations. Unlike many anti-imperialists, however, Orwell never romanticized the Indians or the Burmese he came in contact with. In an otherwise sympathetic portrait of the natives in his novel *Burmese Days* (1933) Orwell created a slimy Burmese villain in U Po Kyin, who for sheer Oriental mendacity is a match for a character such as Fu Manchu.

Orwell returned to England in 1927 and, determined to become a writer, eventually resigned his commission. It would take almost a decade and half before he would earn an income from writing that matched that of his last year as a policeman.

Despite holding a variety of jobs as teacher, storekeeper, and bookstore manager, Orwell wrote incessantly although often without great popular or financial success. Beginning in 1933 he published a book a year for seven years: four novels, one book of semi-autobiography (*Down and Out in Paris and London* [1933]), one piece of brilliant investigative journalism (*The Road to Wigan Pier* [1936]) and the best single book on the Spanish Civil War (*Homage to Catalonia* [1938]), all produced while Orwell worked full time at other jobs. He also wrote book reviews for a number of English journals and began to hone the mastery of the essay that was to make him the greatest practitioner of this deceptively difficult literary form in the first half of the twentieth century. Two of his essays written during these years, 'A Hanging' (1931) and 'Shooting an Elephant' (1936), define the modern essay form. They are direct, powerful, brief studies that stay with the reader for years. . . .

Although most of Orwell's early books were reviewed positively, only *The Road to Wigan Pier* was a financial success. It was commissioned by the successful publisher Victor Gollancz and later adopted by the Left Book Club controlled by him. It sold around 47,000 copies in various editions, a large figure for its day. *The Road to Wigan Pier* also revealed a side of Orwell that was to make him controversial. Gollancz wanted and got a brilliant depiction of the evils of capitalism in Orwell's portrait of the English coal mining industry in the midst of the depression, but he also received a shock. The second half of the book contained a sustained attack on the failures of socialism and socialists. In order to make the case for socialism, Orwell found it necessary to start by attacking its flaws. As with Christianity, he shrewdly noted, 'the worst advertisement for Socialism is its adherents'.

Orwell ridiculed the pretensions and idiosyncrasies of English socialism in an oft-quoted passage in *The Road to Wigan Pier*. 'One sometimes gets the impression that the mere words 'Socialism' and 'Communism' draw towards them with magnetic force every fruit-juice drinker, nudist, sandal-wearer, sex-maniac, Quaker, 'Nature Cure' quack, pacifist and feminist in England'. Harsh, even unfair, but containing just enough truth to hit home.

Orwell knew that Socialism was an overwhelmingly middle class movement. Fascinated with working class values and life styles, he tried to immerse himself into the ranks of the working class after his return from Burma. But he knew that he had failed. This blending of middle and lower classes was a theme that obsessed him for years. He believed overcoming class barriers in England was almost impossible and that Socialism would succeed only when Socialists truly lost their sense of class superiority and became one with the working

An actor wears the "Napoleon the Pig" costume during rehearsal for a stage version of George Orwell's Animal Farm *in Beijing, China, on November 12, 2002.* Peter Parks/AFP/ Getty Images.

class. At the end of *Road to Wigan Pier*, he wrote, half in jest, after all 'we have nothing to lose but our aitches'. Although Orwell's book was resented by some in Wigan, now it has become the focus of the city's tourist appeal. The city has just spent £4 million rebuilding Wigan Pier and tired tourists can visit the Orwell pub.

An Unorthodox Socialist

Orwell followed *The Road to Wigan Pier* with his exposé of the betrayal of the idea of revolution in the Spanish Civil War. For this apostasy, he was a marked man in certain left-wing circles even though Orwell, unlike many of his critics, had actually fought in Spain. In *Homage to Catalonia* (1938), Orwell argued that [Soviet dictator Joseph] Stalin and his allies in Spain were not really interested in a victory for the Republic but rather in prolonging the Civil War as a way of weakening the western democracies. For stating this view that is now accepted by most scholars, Orwell was ostracized by many on the left. Gollancz, for example, refused to publish *Homage to Catalonia*. At the same time Kingsley Martin, editor of the *New Statesman*, the leading left-wing political journal in Britain, had asked Orwell to review a new book on the Spanish Civil War. When Orwell's review contradicted the Popular Front line of 'no enemies on the left', Martin rejected it. Orwell never forgave Martin and accused him of having the 'mentality of a whore'. Years later Malcolm Muggeridge was having lunch with Orwell when the latter asked him to change seats. Why, Muggeridge asked? Orwell said that Martin was sitting nearby, and he could not abide looking at his corrupt face.

Despite his problems with his Socialist friends, Wigan Pier and Spain completed Orwell's conversion to Socialism and he remained a committed, if slightly eccentric, one for the rest of his life. His writing after Spain—save for one last and quite good novel, *Coming Up for Air* (1939) about an England on the eve of war—was overwhelmingly political in nature. In his essay, 'Why I Write', Orwell argued that from 1936 on (i.e., from the time of *Road to Wigan Pier* and the Spanish Civil War), 'I wanted to make political writing into an art'. In this he largely succeeded.

World War II energized him. During the dangerous summer of 1940 when Britain's fate hung in the balance, Orwell rediscovered his latent patriotism. He even tried to join the military but was rejected for health reasons, i.e., he suffered from a serious weakness of the lungs that eventually developed into the tuberculosis that killed him at age 46.

In a sense Orwell enjoyed the war, its dangers, and its privations. He argued that the war had created a unique opportunity for revolutionary Socialism to triumph: both the middle and lower classes were patriots at heart, he thought, and both groups saw the importance of saving England. He argued the case in a long, brilliant essay, 'The Lion and the Unicorn'. Patriotism, Orwell wrote, is the glue that binds the different classes of the English people. England, he argued in a famous analogy, is not Shakespeare's jewelled isle. 'It resembles a family, a rather stuffy Victorian family. It has rich relations who have to be kow-towed to and poor relations who are horribly sat upon. It is a family in which the young are generally thwarted and most of the power is in the hands of irresponsible uncles and bedridden aunts. Still, it is a family. It has its private language and its common memories, and at the approach of an enemy it closes its ranks'.

Two Primary Concerns

By 1942 Orwell recognized that his hope for a great revolution in the midst of the war was a forlorn hope. The last years of his life revolved around two all-consuming fears. First he feared that the future would be controlled by all-powerful totalitarian states in a perpetual state of war. This terror was the genesis of *Nineteen Eighty-Four*, a novel that projected the ghastly post-war age of austerity into the near future.

At least as important as this concern was Orwell's second belief that the very concept of truth was disappearing under the strain of war and propaganda. His experience in Spain when he saw how ideology could corrupt historical events profoundly worried him. He was haunted by memories of how the war news from Spain had been distorted. 'I saw newspaper reports which did not bear any relation to the facts. I saw great battles reported where there had been no fighting, and complete silence where hundreds of men had been killed. I saw, in fact, history being written not in terms of what happened but of what ought to have happened according to various 'party lines'. *Animal Farm* and *Nineteen Eighty-Four*, both partially about how the idea of revolution is betrayed, also deal with the corruption of language and the fading of historical truth. In recent months there has been renewed criticism of Orwell from some left-wing circles in Britain because he had provided a list of pro-Soviet intellectuals to the British security services. Orwell did this because of his fear that a Soviet victory in the Cold War could lead to a totalitarian dictatorship. In our present debates about Iraq, the name of Orwell is heard from all sides. As one Wisconsin newspaper [*The Capital Times*] put it: 'Our time is still George Orwell's time! The year may be 2003, but never in history has the clock ticked more Orwellian than it ticks at this moment'.

Although Orwell died at the height of the Cold War and in the early stages of the break-up of European imperialism, his insights still have validity today. His warnings about trends in totalitarianism are still with us, and his concerns for the vitality of the language are more valid today with the onslaughts of politics and advertising more dangerous than ever before. Orwell remains for the twenty-first century both a man of his time and a man for our time.

Politics in *Animal Farm*

Animal Farm: An Allegory of Revolution

Valerie Meyers

Valerie Meyers is an author and literary critic. With Jeffrey Meyers, she is the author of George Orwell: An Annotated Bibliography of Criticism.

George Orwell uses the literary form of the beast-fable to write Animal Farm, *his critique of communism in Soviet Russia. All of the animals in* Animal Farm *portray specific individuals or groups in Russian history, and the events in the novel represent events in Russian history, according to Valerie Meyers in the following essay. Orwell's purpose in writing the book, Meyers contends, was to expose the rise of totalitarianism in Russia under the former revolutionaries.*

'*A*nimal Farm', Orwell wrote, 'was the first book in which I tried, with full consciousness of what I was doing, to fuse political purpose and artistic purpose into one whole'. In his preface to the Ukrainian edition, published in 1947, Orwell said that he wanted to write the book in a simple language because he wanted to tell ordinary English people, who had enjoyed a tradition of justice and liberty for centuries, what a totalitarian system was like. His experience in Spain had shown him 'how easily totalitarian propaganda can control the opinion of enlightened people in democratic countries' and he wrote the book to destroy the 'Soviet myth' that Russia was a truly socialist society.

In the 1930s European intellectuals idealised the Soviet Union. Even E.M. Forster, a relatively non-political writer, commented in an essay of 1934, 'no political creed except communism offers an intelligent man any hope'. Throughout the 1930s Orwell had been sceptical about the Soviet version of current events in Russia; in Spain he saw Spanish Communists, directed by Moscow, betray their allies. In the late 1930s news reached the West of the infamous Purge Trials, which took the lives of three million people and sent countless others to forced labour camps in order to make [Soviet leader Joseph] Stalin's power absolute. In 1939 Stalin signed a non-aggression pact with [Adolf] Hitler, which allowed the Germans to overrun Poland and Czechoslovakia. Orwell's indignant reaction to these events provoked him to write this powerful pamphlet.

The Genre of *Animal Farm*

Orwell particularly valued the vigorous, colourful and concrete style of pamphlets and wanted to revive the genre. *Animal Farm* was his contribution to the English tradition of Utopian pamphlets, which originated in Thomas More's *Utopia* (1516). Like *Utopia*, *Animal Farm* is brief, light and witty, but has a serious purpose. More's pamphlet attacked the monarch's excessive power and the cruel dispossession of tenant-farmers by the lords who enclosed lands for sheep-grazing; Orwell's attacks the injustice of the Soviet regime and seeks to correct Western misconceptions about Soviet Communism. . . .

More raised the fundamental question, which Orwell took up centuries later, of whether it is possible for men to live together fairly, justly and equally. More's answer is ethical: that there is no point in changing our social system unless we change our morality; his pamphlet urges us to take responsibility for improving our society. While More's Utopia is totally imaginary, Orwell's Animal Farm is based on the first thirty years of the Soviet Union, a real society pursuing the ideal of equality. His book argues that this kind of society hasn't worked, and couldn't.

Orwell said that Jonathan Swift's *Gulliver's Travels* (1726) 'has meant more to me than any other book ever written'. Far longer and more complex than *Utopia*, it uses the same device of a traveller's tales to attack contemporary society, but the various places Gulliver visits are satiric renderings of aspects of English society. Orwell's Animal Farm, like Swift's Lilliput and Blefuscu, is a coded satiric portrait of a real society, an anti-utopia which, by castigating real evils, suggests what society ought to be like. . . .

The Political Allegory

Orwell's critique of Soviet Communism is a beast-fable, a satiric form in which animals are used to represent human vice and folly. [Geoffrey] Chaucer's 'Nun's Priest's Tale', one of the *Canterbury Tales*, is an early example in English. On one level Chaucer's tale is a comic farmyard tale of a proud cock, Chanticleer, who falls prey to the fox and manages to escape; on another it is a witty and learned essay on the significance of dreams; on another, and more serious, level it is an allegory of the Fall of Man, in which Chanticleer represents Adam being tempted by the Devil. *Animal Farm*, a brief, concentrated satire, subtitled 'A Fairy Story', can also be read on the simple level of plot and character. It is an entertaining, witty tale of a farm whose oppressed animals, capable of speech and reason, overcome a cruel master and set up a revolutionary government. They are betrayed by the evil power-hungry pigs, especially by their leader, Napoleon, and forced to return to their former servitude. Only the leadership has changed. On another, more serious level, of course, it is a political allegory, a symbolic tale where all the events and characters represent events and characters in Russian history since 1917, in which 'the interplay between surface action and inner meaning is everything'. Orwell's deeper purpose is to teach a political lesson.

As he noted in his Ukrainian preface, Orwell used actual historical events to construct his story, but rearranged them to fit his plot. Manor Farm is Russia, Mr Jones the Tsar, the pigs the Bolsheviks who led the revolution. The humans represent the ruling class, the animals the workers and peasants. Old Major, the white boar who inspires the rebellion in the first chapter, stands for a combination of [Karl] Marx, the chief theorist, and [Vladimir] Lenin, the actual leader. Orwell makes Old Major a character whose motives are pure and idealistic, to emphasise the positive goals of the revolution, and makes him die before the rebellion itself. In actuality Lenin died in 1924, well after the revolution. Lenin himself set up the machinery of political terror which Stalin took over. The power struggle between Stalin and [Leon] Trotsky (which Orwell satirises in chapter 5) happened after Lenin's death, not immediately after the revolution, as Orwell's account suggests.

The *Communist Manifesto* (1848) of Karl Marx and Friedrich Engels provided a theoretical basis for the revolutionary movements springing up in Europe in the latter part of the nineteenth century. Marx interpreted all history as the history of class struggle, arguing that the capitalist classes, or bourgeoisie, the owners of the means of production, are inevitably opposed to the interests of the wage-earning labourers, or proletariat, whom they exploit. This eternal conflict can only be resolved by revolution, when workers take over the means of production, share the fruits of their labours equally, and set up 'the dictatorship of the proletariat'. Marx's ideal was an international brotherhood of workers (for he believed that the interests of the working classes of all nations would unite them, causing them to cross barriers of race and culture, against the common enemy) and a future classless society. Old Major's speech in the first chapter parodies the ideas of the *Communist Manifesto*. He says: 'Only get rid of Man, and the produce of our labour would be our own.' Their goal should be the 'overthrow of the human race': in the coming struggle

'All men are enemies. All animals are comrades.' In chapter 3 'everyone worked according to his capacity', an echo of the Marxist slogan, 'From each according to his abilities, to each according to his needs.'

Representative of Russian History

Each animal stands for a precise figure or representative type. The pigs, who can read and write and organise, are the Bolshevik intellectuals who came to dominate the vast Soviet bureaucracy. Napoleon is Stalin, the select group around him the Politburo, Snowball is Trotsky, and Squealer represents the propagandists of the regime. The pigs enjoy the privileges of belonging to the new ruling class (special food, shorter working hours), but also suffer the consequences of questioning Napoleon's policies.

The other animals represent various types of common people. Boxer the carthorse (whose name suggests the Boxer Rebellion of 1900, when revolutionaries tried to expel foreigners from China), is the decent working man, fired by enthusiasm for the egalitarian ideal, working overtime in the factories or on the land, willing to die to defend his country; Clover is the eternal, motherly working woman of the people. Molly, the unreliable, frivolous mare, represents the White Russians who opposed the revolution and fled the country; the dogs are the vast army of secret police who maintain Stalin in power; the sheep are the ignorant public who repeat the latest propaganda without thinking and who can be made to turn up to 'spontaneous demonstrations' in support of Napoleon's plans. Moses, the raven, represents the opportunist Church. He flies off after Mr Jones, but returns later, and continues to preach about the Sugarcandy Mountain (or heaven), but the pigs' propaganda obliterates any lingering belief. Benjamin the donkey, the cynical but powerless average man, never believes in the glorious future to come, and is always alert to every betrayal.

Orwell's allegory is comic in its detailed parallels: the hoof and horn is clearly the hammer and sickle, the Communist party emblem; 'Beasts of England' is a parody of the 'Internationale', the party song; the Order of the Green Banner is the Order of Lenin, and the other first- and second-class awards spoof the fondness of Soviet Russia for awarding medals, for everything from exceeding one's quota on the assembly line or in the harvest to bearing a great many children. The poem in praise of Napoleon imitates the sycophantic verses and the mass of paintings and sculptures turned out to glorify Stalin. In chapter 8, Squealer's presentation of impressive figures to show that food production had gone up, and the thin layer of grain sprinkled over the sacks to deceive Whymper, the agent, correspond to the well-known practice in totalitarian regimes of falsifying figures to project a positive image abroad.

Each event of the story has a historical parallel. The Rebellion in chapter 2 is the October 1917 Revolution, the Battle of the Cowshed in chapter 4 the subsequent Civil War. Mr Jones and the farmers represent the loyalist Russians and foreign forces who tried, but failed, to dislodge the Bolsheviks. The hens' revolt in chapter 7 stands for the brutally suppressed 1921 mutiny of the sailors at Kronstadt, which challenged the new regime to release political prisoners and grant freedoms of speech and the press. Napoleon's deal with Whymper, who trades the farm's produce at Willingdon market, represents Russia's 1922 Treaty of Rapallo with Germany. Orwell emphasises Napoleon's decision to trade because it breaks the First Commandment, that 'whatever goes upon two legs is an enemy'. Official Soviet policy was hostile to Germany, a militaristic, capitalist nation, but the Treaty revealed that the Communist regime had been trading arms and heavy machinery, and would continue to do so.

Mr Frederick of 'Pinchfield', renowned for his cruelty to animals and for appropriating others' land, represents Hitler, though his name also suggests the despotic eighteenth-century Prussian king Frederick the Great. Mr Pilkington of 'Foxwood' stands for [Winston] Churchill and England, a country dominated by the fox-hunting upper classes. The Windmill stands for the first Five-Year Plan of 1928, which called for rapid industrialisation and collectivisation of agriculture. Its destruction in a storm in chapter 6 symbolises the grim failure of this policy. Chapter 7 describes in symbolic terms the famine and starvation which followed. The hens' revolt stands for the peasants' bitter resistance to collective farming, when they burned their crops and slaughtered their animals. The animals' false confessions in chapter 7 are the Purge Trials of the late 1930s. The false banknotes given by Frederick for the corn represent Hilter's betrayal of the Nazi-Soviet Pact of 1939, and the second destruction of the Windmill, by Frederick's men, is the Nazi invasion of Russia in 1941. The last chapter brings Orwell up to the date of the book's composition. He ends with a satiric portrait of the Teheran Conference of 1943, the meeting of Churchill, [Franklin Delano] Roosevelt and Stalin, who are now allies. The quarrel over cheating at cards predicts the falling-out of the superpowers as soon as the war ended.

Orwell's Literary Devices

Animal Farm's apparent simplicity disguises Orwell's ingenuity in fitting all these complex historical events into a simple and persuasive plot. Like the three wishes of a fairy tale, the Seven Commandments are an effective structural device. Their stage-by-stage alteration charts the pigs' progressive rise to power and lends the narrative a tragic inevitability. This change also symbolises a key theme of the book: the totalitarian falsification of history. The pigs' gradual acquisition of privileges— apples, milk, house, whisky, beer, clothes—leads to the final identification of pig and human, Communist and capitalist.

The plot's circular movement, which returns the animals to conditions very like those in the beginning, provides occasions for vivid irony. In the first chapter they lament their forced labour and poor food, but by chapter 6 they are starving, and are forced to work once more. In chapter 1 Old Major predicts that one day Jones will send Boxer to the knacker, and in chapter 9 Napoleon fulfils the prophecy by sending him to the slaughterhouse. In chapter 7, when various animals falsely confess their crimes and are summarily executed by the dogs, 'the air was heavy with the smell of blood, which had been unknown there since the expulsion of Jones'. These ironies all emphasise the tragic failure of the revolution, and support Benjamin's view that 'life would go on as it had always gone on—that is, badly'.

Though all the characters are types, Orwell differentiates the two most important figures, Napoleon and Snowball, so that they resemble their real-life counterparts both in the broad lines of their characterisation and in their two major disagreements. Like Stalin, Napoleon 'has a reputation for getting his own way', takes charge of indoctrinating the young, sets up an elaborate propaganda machine, cultivates an image of omnipotent, charismatic power (a 'personality cult'), surrounding himself with bodyguards and fawning attendants. Like Trotsky, Snowball is an intellectual, who quickly researches a topic and formulates plans; he is a persuasive orator, but fails to wrest the leadership from Napoleon. . . .

The beast-fable is not only a device that allows Orwell's serious message to be intelligible on two levels; the use of animal to represent man is basic to his whole theme. We can readily grasp that animals are oppressed and feel it is wrong to exploit them and betray their trust. Orwell counts on our common assumptions about particular species to suggest his meaning. The sheep and their bleating are perfect metaphors for a gullible public, ever ready to accept policies and repeat rumours as truth. We commonly believe pigs are greedy and savage, even to the point of devouring their young. Orwell also uses the natural animosity of cats to sparrows, dogs to rats, to suggest the social and ethnic conflicts which belie Marx's dictum that workers' common interests outweigh differences of race and nationhood. And, most central to his theme, their 'short animal lives' suggests the book's tragic vision: that the passivity and ignorance of ordinary people allows an evil leadership to stay in power.

Orwell wanted his central figure to typify the modern dictator, whose lust for power is pathological and inhuman. Napoleon's swift, secret cruelty makes the other animals seem all too human in comparison. . . .

The beast-fable form not only allowed Orwell to convey a complex message in simple terms, but was also admirably suited to his habits as a writer: his tendency to reduce characters to type, to see society as groups of competing economic interests; his narrator's detachment from the characters; his preference for grammatically simple sentences and unpretentious vocabulary. The prose succeeds brilliantly at balancing entertainment and argument because Orwell blends homely, even clichéd, language with sophisticated diction. In chapter 3, for example, 'the work of the farm went like clockwork' when the animals were in charge; into this simple fabric Orwell inserts a word with Marxist overtones: 'with the worthless *parasitical* human beings gone there was more for everyone to eat. The context makes the word perfectly comprehensible to someone who does not know its meaning, yet if we know the word we can appreciate an additional layer of meaning—the suggestion that the animals have been indoctrinated with the Marxist view of capitalists as parasites, who own the means of production but do no work. The pleasure of reading *Animal Farm* lies in recognising the double meanings, the political and historical parallels, in the story.

In a book where distortion of language is an important theme, every word counts. Orwell's simple language points out the absurd contradictions between public political statements and private perceptions of their meaning. In chapter 6

Tony Flynn as Squealer, Neil Salvage as Benjamin, Claire Storey as Muriel, Rebecca Jackson as Mollie Minimus, and Sarah Groarke as Clover in Peter Hall's stage adaptation of Orwell's Animal Farm at Theatre Royal in Bath, England, in July 2007. © Donald Cooper/Photostage.

all extra work is voluntary, but animals who refuse to do it lose half their rations; in chapter 9 Squealer announces a 'readjustment' of rations, instead of the more accurate 'reduction'. This doubletalk culminates in the last chapter, when the Commandments are reduced to one: 'All animals are equal' now has added to it 'but some are more equal than others'. The comic effect of these verbal distinctions does not diminish the tragedy of the revolution betrayed. . . .

Orwell's Critique of Marx

Orwell had always been fascinated by the corrupting effects of power and the relative weakness of good and decent people in the face of evil intelligence. In *Animal Farm* Orwell argues that, however desirable the ideal, man's instinct for power makes the classless society impossible. In his allegory, a Marxist revolution is doomed to fail, because it grants power, once again, to a select few. Major's speech 'had given to *the more intelligent animals. . .* a completely different outlook on life'.

To oppose Marx, Orwell turned to a classic seventeenth-century work of political philosophy, Thomas Hobbes's *Leviathan* (1651). A fiercely anti-revolutionary writer, Hobbes presents views of man and politics diametrically opposed to those of Marx. According to Hobbes, the life of man is 'solitary, poor, nasty, brutish and short', and all human beings are inclined to 'a perpetual and restless desire after power, which ceaseth only in death'. Far from seeing men as capable of creating a new society to ensure their equality, Hobbes thought that only fear of death made men control their lust for power sufficiently to band together to form a commonwealth, an artificial machine to protect them from their enemies. For Hobbes, the one requirement of government, of whatever kind, was that it be strong enough to hold warring factions in check. He considered it inevitable that society be divided into social classes.

There are several important echoes of Hobbes in *Animal Farm*. Ironically, Marx-Major paraphrases Hobbes in the first chapter, when he says, 'our lives are miserable, laborious, and short'. In the last chapter, when the animals can no longer remember the promises of the revolution, Benjamin expresses the Hobbesian opinion that 'hunger, hardship and disappointment . . . [are] the unalterable law of life'. Alone of all the animals, Benjamin refuses either to hope or be disappointed, and his commentary often suggests a Swiftian cynicism, such as when he refuses to read, on the ground that there is nothing worth reading. This choice turns out to be the wise one, when we consider how the written word has been manipulated by the pigs.

But we should not assume that Benjamin's voice represents Orwell's. Orwell did not agree with Hobbes's political philosophy, nor did he, like Swift, find mankind ultimately disgusting. He simply believed that the rise of Russian totalitarianism could best be explained by Hobbes's theory, rather than by Marx's. . . .

Orwell's book does not pretend to be a probing analysis of Russian Communism. His purpose was to expose the totalitarian nature of the Russian government in as simple and effective a form as possible, and in this he succeeded. It is a cautionary tale, but what it suggests about power and revolution is not reducible to a formula.

As for the criticism that Orwell's satire is exaggerated, the book's continued popularity (in illegal editions) in Eastern Europe shows that his satire is as accurate as it is enduring. As recently as September 1987, customs officials at the Moscow International Book Fair cleared the British exhibitors' shelves of *Animal Farm*. There can be no better certification of its truth.

Orwell Distorts Russian History in *Animal Farm*

Kingsley Martin

British journalist Kingsley Martin was the editor of the left-wing magazine New Statesman and Nation *from 1930 to 1960.*

Kingsley Martin earned Orwell's wrath in 1937 when he refused to publish any of Orwell's articles on the Spanish Civil War because of their criticism of the role of Communists in that war. A number of years later, Orwell asked a luncheon companion to change places with him so that he would not have Martin's "corrupt face" in his view while dining. Given this personal history, it is not surprising that Martin's review of Animal Farm *is dismissive of the novel. Although admitting that* Animal Farm *is well written, Martin accuses Orwell of ignoring the complexity of Russian history. Orwell is a disillusioned idealist, Martin argues, who constantly looks for new ideologies to attack. Instead of his ill-founded attacks on communism, Martin asserts, Orwell should be looking for solutions to the problems of the world.*

In a world choked everywhere with suffering, cruelty and exploitation, the disillusioned idealist may be embarrassed by the rich choice of objects for denunciation. He runs the risk of twisting himself into knots, as he discovers enemies, first to the Right, then to the Left and, most invigorating, at home amongst his friends. He may try to solve his dilemma by deciding on some particular Power-figure as the embodiment of Evil, concentrating upon it all his wealth of frustration and righteous indignation. If he remains only a critic and fails to turn his talent to the search for a practical remedy for a specific evil, he is likely, in time, to decide that all the world is

Kingsley Martin, "*Animal Farm*," in *New Statesman and Nation*, September 8, 1945, pp. 165–166.

evil and that human nature is itself incorrigible. The alternatives then—we see many contemporary instances—are cynicism or religion and mysticism.

Orwell Is an Idealist Turned Cynic

Mr Orwell's Devils have been numerous and, since he is a man of integrity, he chooses real evils to attack. His latest satire, beautifully written, amusing and, if you don't take it too seriously, a fair corrective of much silly worship of the Soviet Union, suggests to me that he is reaching the exhaustion of idealism and approaching the bathos of cynicism. He began as a civil servant, honestly indignant with the misdeeds of the British Empire as he saw it in the Far East. During the Spanish war, a sincere anti-Fascist, he found, like many others of his temperament, that of all the warring groups the most idealistic and least smirched were the anarchists. The fact that they would infallibly have lost the war while the Republican coalition might, in slightly more favourable circumstances, have won it, did not affect his onslaught. At the outset of the World War he repented his past. Realising that Nazi Germany was now an even worse enemy than the British Empire or the [Spanish Communist leader Juan] Negrin Government, he wrote denouncing the Left, scarcely noticing that it was his own back he was lashing, and that his blows often fell short of others who had not made the mistakes with which he charged them. Now that Germany is defeated, it seems almost accidental that his righteous indignation is turned not, say, against the Americans for their treatment of Negroes, but against the Soviet Union. In [Joseph] Stalin he finds the latest incarnation of Evil.

There is plenty in the U.S.S.R. to satirise, and Mr Orwell does it well. How deftly the fairy story of the animals who, in anticipation of freedom and plenty, revolt against the tyrannical farmer, turns into a rollicking caricature of the Russian Revolution! His shafts strike home. We all know of the sheep,

Snowball (played by Greg Hicks) attacks Mr Jones in Peter Hall's stage adaptation of Orwell's Animal Farm *at the Olivier Theatre and National Theatre in London, September 1984.* © Donald Cooper/Photostage.

who drown discussion by the bleating of slogans; we have all noticed, with a wry smile, the gradual change of Soviet doctrine under the pretence that it is no change and then that the original doctrine was an anti-Marxist error. (The best thing in Mr Orwell's story is the picture of the puzzled animals examining the Original Principles of the Revolution, and finding them altered: 'All animals are equal,' said the slogan: to which is added, 'but some are more equal than others.') The falsehoods about [Leon] Trotsky, whose part in the revolutionary period, only secondary to [Vladimir] Lenin's, has been gradually erased from the Soviet history books, is another fair count against Stalinite methods. The story of the loyal horse who worked until his lungs burst and was finally sent off to the knackers' yard is told with a genuine pathos; it represents a true and hateful aspect of every revolutionary struggle. Best of all is the character of the donkey who says little, but is always sure that the more things change the more they will be the same, that men will always be oppressed and exploited whether they have revolutions and high ideals or not.

Orwell's Real Target

The logic of Mr Orwell's satire is surely the ultimate cynicism of Ben, the donkey. That, if I read Mr Orwell's mind correctly, is where his idealism and disillusion has really landed him. But he has not quite the courage to see that he has lost faith, not in Russia but in mankind. So the surface moral of his story is that all would have gone well with the revolution if the wicked Stalin had not driven the brave and good Trotsky out of Eden. Here Mr Orwell ruins what should have been a very perfect piece of satire on human life. For by putting the Stalin-Trotsky struggle in the centre he invites every kind of historical and factual objection. We are brought from the general to the particular; to the question why Stalin decided to attempt the terrific feat of creating an independent Socialist country rather than risk plunging Russia unprepared into a war of intervention by stirring up revolution in neighbouring countries. Mr Orwell may say it would have been better if this policy had prevailed, but a moment's thought will evoke in him the brilliant satire he would have written about the betrayal of the revolution, if Trotsky, who was as ruthless a revolutionary as Stalin, had won the day and lost the revolution by another route. This same error compels the reader to ask whether in fact it is true that the Commissar to-day is indistinguishable in ideals and privilege from the Tzarist bureaucrat and the answer is that though many traditional Russian characteristics survive in Russia, the new ruling class is really very different indeed from anything that Russia has known before. In short, if we read the satire as a gibe at the failings of the U.S.S.R. and realise that it is historically false and neglectful of the complex truth about Russia, we shall enjoy it and be grateful for our laugh. But which will Mr Orwell do next? Having fired his bolt against Stalin, he could return to the attack on British or American Capitalism as seen through the eyes say, of an Indian peasant; the picture would be about as true or as false. Alternatively, there is the Church of Rome,

Yogi, or at a pinch, the more tedious effort to help find the solution of any of the problems that actually face Stalin, [British prime minister Clement] Attlee, Mr Orwell and the rest or us.

Animal Farm Misses the Point About Soviet Communism

Northrop Frye

Northrop Frye (1912–1991) was an author and professor. One of the foremost literary critics of his time, he wrote two major works on literature, Fearful Symmetry *and* Anatomy of Criticism.

In the following review of Animal Farm, *Northrop Frye finds the ending, when the pigs turn into humans, to be a gratuitous device that erroneously implies that Communism has created a society just like life under the czar. He calls this conclusion nonsense. Frye accuses Orwell of taking the easy path, rather than presenting a serious examination of the reasons why the underlying spirit of Marxism had been perverted in practice in the Soviet Union.*

George Orwell's satire on Russian Communism, *Animal Farm*, has just appeared in America, but its fame has preceded it, and surely by now everyone has heard of the fable of the animals who revolted and set up a republic on a farm, how the pigs seized control and how, led by a dictatorial boar named Napoleon, they finally became human beings walking on two legs and canting whips just as the old Farmer Jones had done. At each stage of this receding revolution one of the seven principles of the original rebellion becomes corrupted, so that "no animal shall kill any other animal" has added to it the words "without cause" when there is a great slaughter of the so-called sympathizers of an exiled pig named Snowball, and "no animal shall sleep in a bed" takes on "with sheets" when the pigs move into the human farmhouse and monopo-

Northrop Frye, "Turning New Leaves," *Canadian Forum*, vol. XXVI, no. 311, December 1946, pp. 211–212. Reproduced by permission of the Literary Estate of the author, Victoria University, Toronto.

lize its luxuries. Eventually there is only one principle left, modified to "all animals are equal, but some are more equal than others," as Animal Farm, its name changed back to Manor Farm, is welcomed into the community of human farms again after its neighbors have realized that it makes its "lower" animals work harder on less food than any other farm, so that the model worker's republic becomes a model of exploited labor.

Both Well-Written and Silly

The story is very well-written, especially the Snowball episode, which suggests that the Communist "Trotskyite" [follower of Leon Trotsky] is a conception on much the same mental plane as the Nazi "Jew," and the vicious irony of the end of Boxer the work horse is perhaps really great satire. On the other hand, the satire on the episode corresponding to the German invasion seems to me both silly and heartless, and the final metamorphosis of pigs into humans at the end is a fantastic disruption of the sober logic of the tale. The reason for the change in method was to conclude the story by showing the end of Communism under [Joseph] Stalin as a replica of its beginning under the Czar. Such an alignment is, of course, complete nonsense, and as Mr. Orwell must know it to be nonsense, his motive for adopting it was presumably that he did not know how otherwise to get his allegory rounded off with a neat epigrammatic finish.

Animal Farm adopts one of the Classical formulas of satire, the corruption of principle by expediency, of which [Jonathan] Swift's *Tale of a Tub* is the greatest example. It is an account of the bogging down of Utopian aspirations in the quicksand of human nature which could have been written by a contemporary of [American humorist] Artemus Ward about one of the co-operative communities attempted in America during the last century. But for the same reason it completely misses the point as a satire on the Russian development of

Marxism, and as expressing the disillusionment which many men of goodwill feel about Russia. The reason for that disillusionment would be much better expressed as the corruption of expediency by principle. For the whole point about Marxism was surely that it was the first revolutionary movement in history which attempted to start with a concrete historical situation instead of vast *a priori* generalizations of the "all men are equal" type, and which aimed at scientific rather than Utopian objectives. [Karl] Marx and [Friedrich] Engels worked out a revolutionary technique based on an analysis of history known as dialectic materialism, which appeared in the nineteenth century at a time when metaphysical materialism was a fashionable creed but which Marx and Engels always insisted was a quite different thing from metaphysical materialism.

Orwell Missed Marxism's Real Changes

Today, in the Western democracies, the Marxist approach to historical and economic problems is, whether he realizes it or not, an inseparable part of the modern educated man's consciousness, no less than electrons or dinosaurs, while metaphysical materialism is as dead as the dodo, or would be if it were not for one thing. For a number of reasons, chief among them the comprehensiveness of the demands made on a revolutionary by a revolutionary philosophy, the distinction just made failed utterly to establish itself in practice as it did in theory. Official Marxism today announces on page one that dialectic materialism is to be carefully distinguished from metaphysical materialism, and then insists from page two to the end that Marxism is nevertheless a complete materialist metaphysic of experience, with materialist answers to such questions as the existence of God, the origin of knowledge and the meaning of culture. Thus instead of including itself in the body of modern thought and giving a revolutionary dynamic to that body, Marxism has become a self-contained dogmatic system, and one so exclusive in its approach to the remainder of modern thought as to appear increasingly antiquated and sectarian. Yet this metaphysical materialism has no other basis than that of its original dialectic, its program of revolutionary action. The result is an absolutizing of expediency which makes expediency a principle in itself. From this springs the reckless intellectual dishonesty which it is so hard not to find in modern Communism, and which is naturally capable of rationalizing any form of action, however ruthless.

A really searching satire on Russian Communism, then, would be more deeply concerned with the underlying reasons for its transformation from a proletarian dictatorship into a kind of parody of the Catholic Church. Mr. Orwell does not bother with motivation: he makes his Napoleon inscrutably ambitious, and lets it go at that, and as far as he is concerned some old reactionary bromide like "you can't change human nature" is as good a moral as any other for his fable. But he like [Arthur] Koestler, is an example of a large number of writers in the Western democracies who during the last fifteen years have done their level best to adopt the Russian interpretation of Marxism as their own world-outlook and have failed.

Orwell's Views on the Soviet Union Changed While Conceiving *Animal Farm*

Alok Rai

Alok Rai is an author and professor in the English Department at the University of Delhi in India.

In the following selection, Alok Rai contends that it is important to understand the background against which Animal Farm *was written to fully appreciate the book. Orwell deliberately wrote a devastating attack on the Soviet Union during World War II, at a time when it was exceedingly unpopular among the Western Allies to criticize their Russian ally. When Orwell conceived of* Animal Farm, *Rai asserts, he was optimistic that the advances he had hoped for under socialism and communism were possible. Rai explains that Orwell's subsequent disillusionment is reflected in* Animal Farm's *satirical portrait of the aftermath of the Russian Revolution.*

The matter of *Animal Farm*, both text and context, is rich in ironies—not all of them, be it said, intentional. *Animal Farm* is, as every schoolboy knows, a brilliant farmyard cartoon of the tragic course of the Russian Revolution. The dreamt-of revolution of the beasts is systematically, cynically, betrayed by operators and tyrants who mouth the rhetoric of equality and liberation. The taciturn Napoleon-[Joseph] Stalin outmanoeuvres the vivacious Snowball-[Leon] Trotsky and drives him into exile. The 'revolution' passes through the familiar processes of distortion and cruelty, episodes of hunger and hardship, frame-ups, confessions, liquidations, ending up

Alok Rai, "The Roads to Airstrip One," *Orwell and the Politics of Despair: A Critical Study of the Writings of George Orwell*, New York, NY: Cambridge University Press, 1988, pp. 113–149. Copyright © Cambridge University Press 1988. Reprinted with the permission of Cambridge University Press.

in the most famous thesis of the betrayed revolution: 'All animals are equal, but some animals are more equal than others.' The historical referents of this fabulous account have been identified often enough—and, at this level, there is little further to be said. The transposition of real historical events, the cruel ironies of a familiar history, into farmyard terms is little short of scintillating. It is also, by the same token, drastically reductive.

Anti-Russian Sentiment Unpopular

Its subsequent and durable popularity has obscured the fact that Orwell's *Animal Farm* was a calculated outrage, a deliberately provocative affront to the contemporary admiration for the Soviet Union, whose armies were fighting with epic heroism against [Adolf] Hitler's dread war machine. This background is crucial to a correct understanding of Orwell's brilliantly serious jest. The wartime popularity of the Soviet Union was an oft-repeated theme in Orwell's BBC broadcasts. Commenting on German anti-Bolshevik propaganda, Orwell went so far as to say that it 'was foredoomed to failure because the anti-Russian sentiment on which the Axis propagandists seem to be playing is almost non-existent in the Anglo-Saxon countries'. However, he thought, such propaganda might find sympathetic listeners 'among the wealthier classes all over Europe'. In his broadcast of 13 June 1942, Orwell welcomed the recently signed Anglo-Russian Treaty about wartime coordination and post-war collaboration: 'the two regimes are now in far greater political and economic agreement than would have been possible or even thinkable five years ago. It means, in fact, that the ancient ghost of Bolshevism and "bloody revolution" has been laid [to rest] for ever.' This new-found respectability of the Soviet Union—as also the popularity— could support several different conclusions. It might, for instance, be seen as an index or factor of the processes that conduced towards the Labour victory of 1945. Orwell, however, had for several years been of the opinion that the interests of the Soviet Union were antithetical to those of socialism, and the endorsement of the Soviet regime by His Majesty's Government [King George VI] was hardly likely to make him change his mind. He was, thus, surprised by the 'Upper Crust' delight at the dissolution of the Comintern[1] in 1943: 'a fact which I record but cannot readily explain', because, of course, in Orwell's eyes, 'the Comintern has been one of the worst enemies the working class has had.' From his somewhat eccentric location, therefore, raising the 'ancient ghost of Bolshevism' once again, albeit in a left-wing version, could well appear to be a sacred and lonely *socialist* duty.

When first offered for publication in early 1944, *Animal Farm* was so far out of line with prevalent opinion, and official policy, that it nearly ended up not being published at all. Or published, in despair, as a broadsheet by Orwell's impecunious friend, the poet Paul Potts—which might have been very nearly the same thing. The story of the rejections of the *Animal Farm* ms [manuscript] is well known. Cape rejected it on advice from the Ministry of Information, and relayed, in its rejection letter, the 'imbecile' advice that the ms might become more acceptable if the *Animal Farm* elite were depicted not as pigs but as other, less offensive beasts. T.S. Eliot rejected it on behalf of Faber, and Orwell reports an American publisher turning it down on the grounds that 'animal stories did not sell well in the U.S.A.'. Stung by the rejections. Orwell wrote an angry 'preface' to the projected broadsheet which, in the event, was not used because Warburg, finally, decided to publish the unwanted ms. The rest is history. *Animal Farm* became one of the publishing sensations of our time, and Orwell's 'provocation' achieved apotheosis [immortality] as a universal school text. 'If liberty means anything at all'. Orwell wrote in the 'lost' preface, 'The freedom of the press', in early

1. The Comintern (Communist International) was formed in 1919 to establish an international Soviet republic.

1944 when the popularity of the Soviet Union was at its height, 'it means the right to tell people what they do not want to hear.' Ironically enough, it was written in defence of a fable that people never seem to tire of.

Disillusioned with Communism

However, Orwell's achievement in *Animal Farm* is ironic not only in respect of the disjunction between its anticipated un-popularity and its popular success, it is ironic also in respect of the gap between what Orwell had first intended to write, and the fable he actually wrote. Explaining the genesis of *Animal Farm* in the 'Author's preface to the Ukrainian edition of *Animal Farm*', Orwell said:

> if only animals became aware of their strength we should have no power over them . . . I proceeded to analyse Marx's theory from the animals' point of view. To them it was clear that the concept of a class struggle between humans was pure illusion . . . the true struggle is between animals and humans. From this point of departure, it was not difficult to elaborate the story.

It is evident from this that *Animal Farm* had been intended as an allegory of the common people, awaking to a realisation of their strength and overthrowing their oppressors—a sort of farmyard version of [Orwell's essay] *The Lion and the Unicorn*. In working out the fable, however, in the winter of 1943–4, the euphoria ha[d] collapsed. In 1954 a critic suggested that *Animal Farm* was not really about the Russian Revolution but rather about the English 'revolution' which had seemed immi-nent in *The Lion and the Unicorn*. At a superficial level, this is clearly wrong. The tragic course of the Russian Revolution was very much in Orwell's mind in *Animal Farm*, to the ex-tent that he made a correction, at proof stage, in recognition of Stalin's bravery, in the face of the German advance on Mos-cow: when the windmill was blown up, 'all the animals except Napoleon', he insisted, 'flung themselves on their faces'. In an

Joseph Stalin (pictured here) was General Secretary of the Russian Communist Party and leader of the Soviet Union at the time that Animal Farm *was written. Stalin's Great Purge of the Communist Party during the 1930s resulted in the deaths of millions.* AP Images.

unpublished letter to his agent, now in the Berg collection in New York, Orwell wrote: 'If they question you again, please say that *Animal Farm* is intended as a satire on dictatorship in general but *of course* the Russian Revolution is the chief target. It is humbug to pretend anything else.' However, at a deeper level, it is still possible to see that the disappointment of his wartime hopes—his feeling that 'the political advance we seemed to make in 1940 has been gradually filched away from us'—lent its specific accent of anguish and despair to Orwell's critique of the Russian Revolution. In this mood, the grotesque transformation of the Russian Revolution, of which Orwell had been openly critical for some time, became a paradigmatic instance of *all* attempts at revolutionary social transformation.

One unintended effect of Orwell's avowedly leftist critique of the violence and tyranny of the pigs—the post-revolutionary elite—is that the regime of Jones, softened by nostalgia, begins to appear almost prelapsarian [as before the Fall of humankind]. This was *not* an avowal that Orwell could make explicitly. Thus, as the pigs become more ruthless and tyrannical they become, Orwell insists, more like men—like Pilkington and Frederick, like Jones. However, between the men who act like pigs and the pigs who become like men, there is precious little room for the animals who dreamt of revolution—or for the imagination that dreamt that dream. Thus, it is precisely my argument that with his wartime affirmation, the infectious euphoria that ended in disappointment, Orwell has boxed himself in. In this state, Orwell's intended allegory of the spontaneous revolution becomes an allegory of the revolution endlessly betrayed, a perverse and brilliant distillation of the worst features of the Russian Revolution into a sort of supratemporal fatality, an iron destiny of treachery, and despair, and endless anguish, an exuberant and flamboyantly sarcastic prelude to Orwell's final, gloomy masterpiece, *Nineteen Eighty-Four*.

Historical Context Is Vital to Understanding *Animal Farm*

John Rodden

John Rodden, an author and literary critic, is a professor at the University of Texas at Austin and the editor of The Cambridge Companion to George Orwell.

In the following viewpoint, John Rodden suggests that the fall of communism in Eastern Europe and the collapse of the USSR have dramatically changed the way in which Animal Farm *is viewed by twenty-first-century students, who have grown up in a post–Cold War environment. The book works on three levels, Rodden maintains. First,* Animal Farm *is a historical satire about the history of the USSR. Second, it is a treatise that reflects on power, tyranny, and revolution in general. Third, it is a fable with a message about human nature. To fully comprehend the book on all its levels, it is important to have an understanding of Russian history, Rodden insists.*

With the approach of the centennial of George Orwell's birth in June 2003, much attention is already turning to reassessments of his life and to the ongoing relevance in the new millennium of his masterwork, *Nineteen Eighty-Four* (1949). Easily neglected amid the hoopla is the magnificent little beast fable of totalitarianism which launched Orwell's fame and which he often called his "favorite" book, *Animal Farm* (1945). This essay looks at how changing historical conditions have altered the reception of *Animal Farm* in the last decade—since the collapse of the U.S.S.R. in December 1991. My focus is on how differently Orwell's allegory is being en-

John Rodden, "Appreciating *Animal Farm* in the New Millennium," *Modern Age*, vol. 45, no. 1, Winter 2003, pp. 67–76. Copyright © 2003 Intercollegiate Studies Institute Inc. Reproduced by permission.

countered by new generations in the twenty-first century—who are not even old enough to remember the existence of the Soviet Union. . . .

More Than an Animal Story

When George Orwell submitted *Animal Farm* in 1945 to Dial Press in New York, it was rejected with the explanation that "it was impossible to sell animal stories in the USA." The anecdote is comical in hindsight, but the editors at Dial Press were not the only readers of *Animal Farm* to make this mistake. British readers did so, too. Indeed, some British booksellers erroneously placed it in the "Children's Section" of their shops. (Orwell himself had to scurry around London to switch it to the "adult fiction" shelves.) Indeed, many early readers of Orwell's little masterpiece apparently did not realize that it was a brilliant work of political satire. They read the book much as did the young son of the art critic Herbert Read, one of Orwell's friends at the BBC, who reported that his boy "insisted on my reading it, chapter by chapter . . . and he enjoys it innocently as much as I enjoy it maliciously." It does seem absurd to the knowledgeable present-day reader that the literary public of the 1940s could have read *Animal Farm* "innocently," only on the literal level. We think: How could editors and publishers misjudge a sophisticated classic for a children's tale? How could they confuse an ingenious attack targeting the betrayal of revolution in general and the Soviet Union in particular for a simple animal story?

I find that today's college students are liable to make the same error, and the key to understanding their confusions has to do with the language and form of *Animal Farm*. In a certain sense, *Animal Farm* has been victimized by its astonishing success as a political satire. Orwell's "simple" little book is quite "sophisticated"—and liable to deceive readers into taking it too lightly if they are inattentive to the parallels between the story and Soviet history. And these historical issues are themselves anything but "simple."

The fact is that *Animal Farm* works so beautifully on its literal, surface level as an animal story that it may lull the unwary reader into staying on the surface, thereby misleading him or her into missing its underlying political and historical references. Ironically, then, it is a measure of *Animal Farm*'s artistic excellence that it "fools" some readers into taking it for an animal story. The plain language, straightforward plot, and one-dimensional characters mask the complex subject matter and context. *Animal Farm* is simple on the surface and quite subtle beneath it. All readers—like the publishers of the 1940s who rejected the book—think in terms of book categories when they read. We classify books as fiction or nonfiction, biographies or autobiographies—or, to refer to the present example: adult novels or children's tales, series fiction or animal stories. Thus, the essential error of some readers "fooled" by *Animal Farm* has been what Gilbert Ryle termed a "category mistake": they mistake its genre. They see only its surface message, misreading it as nothing more than a children's tale or animal story.

Animal Farm Is Also an Allegory

Indeed, Orwell's little book is both of these—on the surface. But that is not, first and foremost, what it is. As historically informed and artistically alert readers have long appreciated, *Animal Farm* is far more than an uncontroversial little children's book. First, it is a political allegory of the history of the U.S.S.R.—sometimes jokingly referred to as an "animallegory." Traditionally, an allegory is a symbolic tale that treats a spiritual subject under the guise of a worldly one, such as [William] Langland's *Piers Plowman* and [John] Bunyan's *Pilgrim's Progress*.

Secondly, *Animal Farm* is an allegory written in the form of a beast fable, in which the misadventures of animals expose human follies. Orwell draws on our cultural stereotypes of animals: Pigs have a bad name for selfishness and gluttony.

Horses are slow-witted, strong, gentle, and loyal. Sheep are brainless and behave as a flock without individual initiative. Orwell's point of departure for the fable was a statement from Karl Marx's *Economic and Philosophical Manuscripts* of 1844: "The worker in his human functions no longer feels himself to be anything but animal. What is animal becomes human and what is human becomes animal."

Orwell adapts the literary forms of the allegory and beast fable for his own purposes. "The business of making people conscious of what is happening outside their own small circle," he once wrote, "is one of the major problems of our time, and a new literary technique will have to be evolved to meet it." Orwell's symbolic tale takes a political subject and treats it under the guise of an innocent animal story. But *Animal Farm* also has a stinging moral warning against the abuse of power.

Like most allegories, *Animal Farm* operates by framing one-to-one correspondences between the literal and symbolic levels. Its events and characters function as a simple story on the literal level. But they also operate on a symbolic level for readers who know the "code." In this case, the key code is the history of Soviet Communism. Orwell subtitled *Animal Farm* as "a fairy story," but the subtitle was an ironic joke. He meant that his beast fable was no mere "fairy story," but that it was happening in Stalin's Russia, and that it could happen anywhere. Parts of Orwell's "code" are easy to "crack." For instance, the pigs represent the Communist Party. The pig leader Napoleon and his rival Snowball symbolize the dictator [Joseph] Stalin and the Communist leader Leon Trotsky. Old Major is a composite of Karl Marx and Vladimir Ilyich Lenin, the major theorist and the key revolutionary leader of Communism, respectively. "Beasts of England" is a parody of the Internationale, the Communist Party hymn. The animals' rebellion in Chapter 2 represents the Russian Revolution of October 1917. The battle of the Cowshed in Chapter 4 depicts the subsequent civil war. Mr. Jones and the farmers are the loyalist Russians and foreign forces who tried but failed to dislodge the Bolsheviks, the revolutionaries led by Lenin. The animals' false confessions in Chapter 7 represent the purge trials of the late 1930s. Frederick's stratagem to exchange banknotes for corn recalls Hitler's betrayal of the 1939 Nazi-Soviet pact in June 1941. The first demolition of the windmill, which Napoleon blames on his pig rival, Snowball, symbolizes the failure of the first Five-Year Plan, an industrial plan to coordinate the Soviet economy in the 1920s that did not bring prosperity. The second destruction of the windmill by Frederick's men corresponds to the Nazi invasion of Russia in 1941. The meeting of pigs and humans at the end of the story represents the November 1943 wartime conference in Teheran, which Stalin, [U.S. president Franklin] Roosevelt and [British prime minister Winston] Churchill attended.

If a reader misses such allegorical correspondences, he or she may completely misread the book. Moreover, an allegory can work on different levels. These two difficulties account for much of the confusion and controversy about *Animal Farm*. Readers who naively take it as merely an "animal story" miss the allegorical correspondences altogether. Readers who take *Animal Farm* merely as crude propaganda—as a vulgar diatribe against communism (or socialism)—fail to grasp the various levels on which Orwell's allegory is working.

The fact is that *Animal Farm* functions as an allegory on four levels. On the immediate verbal level, it is a children's story about an animal rebellion on a farm. As an animal story, the work invites the reader to respond compassionately to the sufferings of vulnerable beasts. We readers identify with the suffering and oppression of the poor animals.

Indeed, Orwell once explained that a scene of a suffering horse (who later became the model for Boxer) inspired him to conceive *Animal Farm*:

> The actual details of the story did not come to me for some
> time until one day (I was then living in a small village) I

saw a little boy, perhaps ten years old, driving a huge cart-horse along a narrow path whipping it whenever it tried to turn. It struck me that if only such animals became aware of their strength, we should have no power over them, and that men exploit animals in much the same way as the rich exploit the proletariat. I proceeded to analyze Marx's theory from the animals' point of view.

Orwell's last line makes clear the larger purpose of his story. And it suggests the other levels on which the fable functions.

Different Things to Different People

Beyond an explicit, literal level, then, are three symbolic levels on which *Animal Farm* operates. First, it is a historical satire of the Russian Revolution and the subsequent Soviet dictatorship, in which the precision of Orwell's allegory covers exact historical correspondences between the events of *Animal Farm* and Soviet history up to 1943.

Second, *Animal Farm* is a political treatise that suggests larger lessons about power, tyranny, and revolution in general. On this level, Orwell's book has a much broader historical and political message, one that is not limited to criticism of the Soviet Union.

Third, *Animal Farm* is a fable, or a "fairy tale," as Orwell termed it. It carries a universal moral about the "animality" of human nature. For instance, by the conclusion of *Animal Farm*, some of the pigs are walking upright and wearing human clothes: they are little different from corrupt human beings. *Animal Farm* mirrors our human world, which is sometimes referred to as "the human circus" because the various types of human personality can be compared to the character types of animals. Some humans are like pigs, others resemble sheep, still others can be compared to dogs, and so forth. On this level, Orwell's "fable" about human nature transcends both history and particular political events. We see how the

Barrie Rutter as Napoleon (fourth from left) and David Ryall as Squealer (on right) in Peter Hall's stage adaptation of Orwell's Animal Farm *at the Olivier Theatre and National Theatre in London during September 1984.* © Donald Cooper/Photostage.

fundamental characters of animals do not change. The animals behave consistently, whether in a noble or selfish spirit, through all the changes in the story from the feudal, aristocratic, conservative farm run by Mr. Jones to the modern, progressive, radical *"animal farm"* ruled by Napoleon.

If the young son of Herbert Read thought that *Animal Farm* was just an animal story, the reaction of the son of the poet William Empson also suggests the opposite tendency. Empson reported that his boy, a supporter of Britain's Conservative Party, was "delighted" with *Animal Farm* and considered it "very strong Tory [Conservative] propaganda." Empson concluded his letter about *Animal Farm*:

> I read it with great excitement. And then, thinking it over, and especially on showing it to other people, one realizes that the danger of this kind of perfection is that it means very different things to different readers. . . . I certainly don't mean that that is a fault in the allegory. . . . But I thought it worth warning you (while thanking you very heartily) that

you must expect to be "misunderstood" on a large scale about this book; it is a form that inherently means more than the author means, when it is handled sufficiently well.

Thus, the allegorical form, as well as the complexities of international politics, contributed to misunderstandings about *Animal Farm.* Then and later, Orwell's book came to mean many different things to different people.

But some other editors of the 1940s, who saw quite clearly the political dimension of *Animal Farm,* also rejected it precisely for that reason. Indeed that was the major reason why *Animal Farm* was turned down by two dozen British and American publishers before gaining acceptance for publication. (The scarcity of newsprint during wartime was another reason for its rejection by publishers.)

A Changing Political Landscape

Given the wartime alliance among the Allies, some publishers deemed *Animal Farm* far too controversial to be published. Loyal to the united war effort, four British editors rejected *Animal Farm* because they did not want to risk offending the Soviet Union by publishing such a harsh assault on its history. In the U.S., numerous editors turned it down because they were Soviet sympathizers who considered Orwell's attack on the U.S.S.R. unbalanced and exaggerated.

And yet, public opinion in Britain and America changed toward the U.S.S.R. in 1945–1946. As the need for wartime solidarity with the U.S.S.R. ended with the defeat of Germany and Japan, and as Stalin's armies aggressively occupied much of Eastern Europe, the West's cordial attitude toward the U.S.S.R. cooled. Publishers became more and more willing to criticize Stalin, who had been affectionately dubbed "Uncle Joe" during World War II. Now, with the war over, British and American policymakers judged the U.S.S.R. to be their greatest threat.

Ironically, *Animal Farm* now seemed to be a prophetic book, ahead of its time. Orwell seemed to have predicted the collapse of the Allied alliance and unveiled the Soviet dictatorship as the new enemy of Western democracy. *Animal Farm* seemed to forecast the upcoming international face-off: the Cold War between the democratic West and the Communist nations led by the U.S.S.R.

Another twist of ironic fate was at hand for *Animal Farm*. A book that had, just months earlier, been rejected by publishers as either an unmarketable "animal story" or a dangerous political book, became a runaway best-seller.

New Readers, New Misunderstandings

This short overview of the historical and literary issues pertinent to the composition and early reception of *Animal Farm* has contemporary relevance. No less than the early readers of Orwell's book, we today—film viewers as well as readers—are prone to make similar errors about *Animal Farm*. Indeed we are probably far more likely to miss the political dimension of *Animal Farm* or, at minimum, to misunderstand the complex political situation of the 1940s that it directly addresses. For the historical context of *Animal Farm*, which covers a quarter-century ranging from the Russian Revolution (1917) to the Allies' wartime conference in Teheran (1943), is far removed from current issues in American international relations. Lenin and Stalin are little more than names to many young Americans today. Even World War II feels like a vague and distant episode to many Americans, a storybook event that American high school students study about in their textbooks.

My experience is that many young Americans do not even know that the U.S.S.R. ever existed or that it was dissolved a decade ago. Nor are they aware that the former republics of the Soviet Union are now separate, independent nations, with Russia constituting just one of 15 states of a loose confederation of nations known as the Commonwealth of Independent

States. When I have taught *Animal Farm* to high school students and college undergraduates, my challenge has been to bridge the historical gulf between the current American scene and those events in the first half of the twentieth century that constitute the political background of *Animal Farm.*

Probably more so than with most twentieth-century works, it is vital to approach *Animal Farm* with an awareness of this context. As we have seen, the meaning and even the genre of the book are easily misunderstood without a rich appreciation of this context. And that context is rapidly receding now that the twentieth century has passed and we live in the post-Communist era of the so-called New World Order. So anti-Communism as a major political issue in the Western nations is virtually dead.

To appreciate *Animal Farm* today we need to understand how in the first half of the century Communism and anti-Communism were among the most significant issues in American and British political affairs. And to do this, we need to understand the original political background of that period, against which Orwell wrote his book. Although our increasing historical distance makes all that ever more difficult, we also possess the advantage of observing this period from a broader temporal perspective. Now that the Soviet Union has receded into history, the beginning decades of its development are easier to examine in light of new archival materials and apart from the political controversies that earlier generations had to confront.

Orwell's fable is even more valuable for young readers than ever before. *Animal Farm* may promote understanding of the history and international politics of the twentieth century, stimulate classroom discussion of distant historical events, and help explain (albeit in greatly simplified terms) the causes of the rise and fall of the Soviet Union. Viewers, as well as readers, will find that *Animal Farm* captures both the hope and the tragedy of the Russian Revolution, and that it provides an introduction to a few of the major figures in the history of Communism. *Animal Farm* is a fable that offers simple, valuable political lessons. Among them are the following: power corrupts; revolutions tend to come full circle and devour their peoples; and even good, decent people not only hunger for power, but also worship powerful leaders.

Animal Farm will continue, therefore, to serve as an aid to grasping twentieth-century history, both Russian and Western, and for understanding biographical and political issues related to the nature of socialism, the Russian Revolution, Marxist theory, and the abuse of language.

Animal Farm emerged from and has generated political controversy, but it has also sometimes been naively misjudged as unpolitical. Why has it been mired in historical controversy? Why has it been judged to be completely innocent politically? By examining in detail the historical and political context of Orwell's fable, students will better comprehend how and why such extremely opposed views of the book have arisen and will continue to arise (or even increase). . . .

But let us also not forget that George Orwell was a supremely gifted writer who judged *Animal Farm* as his literary masterpiece. As Orwell declared in his essay, "Why I Write": "*Animal Farm* was the first book in which I tried, with full consciousness of what I was doing, to fuse political purpose and artistic purpose into one whole."

Animal Farm Satirizes All Dictatorships

J.R. Hammond

J.R. Hammond was a literary critic, author, and research fellow at Nottingham Trent University in the United Kingdom.

In the following essay, J.R. Hammond argues that Animal Farm *is not simply a satire on the Soviet Union but is also an attack on all totalitarian regimes. He cites evidence from the text to support his position, including the fact that the ruling pig is named Napoleon. Orwell's theme is that power corrupts, and thus all revolutions—no matter which fine principles they begin with—end up as tyrannies. Hammond maintains that this is a universal message and is the reason why* Animal Farm *retains its relevance.*

*[A*nimal Farm] is totally different in style and conception from anything Orwell had previously written. Written in a simple and fluent manner, it is cast in the form of a short narrative describing a group of animals on a farm who, inspired by the teachings of a wise old boar, rebel against the farmer and assume control for themselves. Leadership devolves upon the pigs who direct and supervise the others in the running of the enterprise. At first the animals are guided in their activities by Seven Commandments which 'form an unalterable law by which all the animals on Animal Farm must live for ever after'. Gradually, however, these Commandments are altered or diluted by the pigs to suit their own convenience until they bear little relation to the original tenets. The pigs become increasingly dictatorial and in time arrogate

to themselves the privileges previously exercised by humans. One by one the principles which inspired the original rebellion are abandoned until at last there remains a single Commandment: ALL ANIMALS ARE EQUAL BUT SOME ANIMALS ARE MORE EQUAL THAN OTHERS. By the end of the story the pigs have assumed so many human attributes that they resemble human beings in appearance. The book ends on a note of discord as the pigs invite the neighbouring farmers to a conference and quarrel whilst playing cards:

> Twelve voices were shouting in anger, and they were all alike. No question, now, what had happened to the faces of the pigs. The creatures outside looked from pig to man, and from man to pig, and from pig to man again; but already it was impossible to say which was which.

Parallels with Soviet History

Critical discussion of *Animal Farm* has tended to concentrate largely on its satirical and allegorical elements. Certainly there are close parallels between the plot of the book and the history of the USSR between 1917 and 1943, and the book should be examined carefully for such parallels. The numerous symbolisms may be expressed in tabular form, as [seen in the table "Correspondences Between Animal Farm and the Real World"].

[Correspondences Between Animal Farm and the Real World]

Mr Jones	Tsar Nicholas II
Major	Marx
Boxer	The Proletariat
Napoleon	Stalin
Snowball	Trotsky
Squealer	*Pravda* [official Soviet newspaper]
Minimus	[poet Vladimir] Mayakovsky
The Pigs	The Bolsheviks
Moses	The Russian Orthodox Church
Mollie	The White Russians
Pilkington	Britain

Frederick	Germany
The farmhouse	The Kremlin
The Rebellion	The Russian Revolution
The Battle of	The allied invasion of 1918–19
the Cowshed	
The Battle of the	The German invasion of 1941
Windmill	
The windmill	The Five-Year Plans
'Beasts of England'	'L'Internationale'

The symbolism of the book is remarkably detailed and reveals an impressive knowledge of Soviet history and Marxist theory. The principal events in the history of the USSR are followed in detail and include, for example, the sailors' uprising of 1921 (the revolt of the hens), the collectivisation of 1929–33 (the failure of the crops), the Moscow Trials of 1936–8 (the confession of the pigs), and the Teheran Conference of 1943 (the final conference of pigs and humans). So gentle is the satire, however, that the allegory which provides the story with its *raison d'être* is not obtrusive. It would be entirely possible for a reader unaware of its nuances to approach the narrative simply as an animal fable. Indeed it is on record that one publisher declined to accept the book on the grounds that 'it was impossible to sell animal stories in the U.S.A.'

A Broader Interpretation

Yet it would be too simplistic to interpret *Animal Farm* solely in terms of a satire on the Soviet Union. It is clear from many indications that Orwell had wider aims in mind. In a letter to his agent Leonard Moore he stated that the book 'is intended as a satire on dictatorship in general', and indeed a careful reading of the story reveals a number of pointers to a more generalised interpretation. There is, first, the fact that the ruling pig is named 'Napoleon': a reminder that there have been many dictatorships in history apart from that of Stalin. Then there are a number of characters which are difficult to place in a strict equation with Russian history: Benjamin the donkey, for example, who clearly has a wider relevance than his minor role in the story would immediately suggest. Most significant of all is that the story is not presented as a simple apposition between the pigs and the other animals; all the animals *including the pigs* are deceived by the neighbouring farmers Frederick and Pilkington, whom Napoleon and his followers come more and more to resemble. The regimes of Frederick and Pilkington, then, are no less cynical and debased than that of Napoleon. It is not Communism as such which corrupts Napoleon as much as the relentless accumulation of power. Totalitarianism *per se*, whatever form it may take, is the enemy Orwell had learned to fear and detest and which *Animal Farm* sought to expose.

It is significant that he chose to do this in the form of an animal fable—a literary genre which can be traced back at least to *Aesop's Fables* of the sixth century BC—rather than a conventional or political treatise. If the book was no more than a satirical allegory told in the form of a parable it is doubtful if it would have achieved the extraordinary success it has enjoyed since 1945. Clearly it must possess some intrinsic literary qualities which have encouraged readers to return to it again and again as a story which can be read for enjoyment and not simply for instruction. It is now acknowledged as his most perfectly constructed work, a work of admirable symmetry and unusual imaginative power. How was it done?

Orwell Loved Animals

Its strength lies, I suggest, in two aspects: first, its incomparable success as a beast fable and second, the extremely skilful manner in which language is deployed to achieve the effects the author is striving for.

There is no doubt that animals had a deep appeal for Orwell. In an essay written towards the end of his life, 'Such, Such were the Joys', he wrote: 'Most of the good memories of my childhood and up to the age of about twenty are in some way connected with animals'. As a boy he was very fond of Beatrix Potter's *The Tale of Pigling Bland* and he and a friend would take it in turns to read it aloud. That he was fascinated by animals and their characteristics may be seen from the unusual amount of animal imagery in his novels. To give only four examples: Ma Hla May in *Burmese Days* is described as having 'rather nice teeth, like the teeth of a kitten'; we are told that the expression on the face of Mrs Creevy in *A Clergyman's Daughter* 'sullen and ill-shaped with the lower lip turned down, recalled that of a toad'; Julia Comstock in *Keep the Aspidistra Flying* was 'one of those girls who even at their most youthful remind one irresistibly of a goose'; and Hilda Vincent in *Coming Up For Air* bore 'a distinct resemblance to a hare'. This tendency to attribute non-human characteristics to human beings had its counterpart in an ability to endow farm creatures with human emotions. Much of the appeal of *Animal Farm* stems from the fact that such characters as Boxer, Clover, Benjamin and Mollie are not simply caricatures but wholly believable individuals.

His childhood friend Jacintha Buddicom wrote:

> The only book by George Orwell I had ever seen was *Animal Farm*, but it had impressed me more than anything I had read for years. Of course, once you knew, it was obvious that it could only have been written by Eric [Blair, Orwell's real name]. It was so exactly like him, so exactly the book he would have loved to read if someone else had written it when he was a boy. It is a *beautiful* book.

Throughout his life Orwell loved animals. While living at Wallington he kept goats and hens, and he and his wife invented humorous names for them and related to each other imaginary stories in which the farmyard animals had amusing adventures. The idea of writing a beast fable would also have had a strong appeal for him in view of his deep admiration for such allegorical works as *Gulliver's Travels*. What is so remarkable about *Animal Farm* is the skilful manner in which animal characteristics are portrayed; the animals are not merely symbols but each possesses the traits of its species:

> At the last moment Mollie, the foolish, pretty white mare who drew Mr. Jones's trap, came mincing daintily in, chewing at a lump of sugar. She took a place near the front and began flirting her white mane, hoping to draw attention to the red ribbons it was plaited with. Last of all came the cat, who looked round, as usual, for the warmest place, and finally squeezed herself in between Boxer and Clover; there she purred contentedly throughout Major's speech without listening to a word of what he was saying.

It is a book which could only have been written by an author who liked animals and understood their ways and foibles. Orwell clearly sympathises with the animals at each stage of their experiences: this empathy, this ability to reach inside their minds and describe their thoughts and emotions *as if from the inside* is one of the most attractive features of the story and is one of many reasons why the satire is so successful. A story in which the animals were merely caricatures without individual traits would not have been nearly so effective.

An Effective Genre

The advantage of the beast fable is that it enables a simple message to be conveyed without the distraction of psychological considerations and the subtleties of plot and atmosphere normally inseparable from a novel. It enables an oversimplified picture to be presented, divorced from complex human personalities, which in a satire of this kind would have no place. Since Orwell's strengths were those of an essayist and satirist rather than those of a novelist in the accepted sense the fable provided him with an ideal medium for the presentation of his theme. (It should be noted, however, that simplicity does not necessarily mean unambiguity. *Animal Farm*

Scene from an animated film adaptation of George Orwell's Animal Farm. *The scene shows a pig living in a human house and dining luxuriously, which violates the Seven Command-ments of the constitution set up after the revolution.* The Kobal Collection/The Picture Desk, Inc.

was interpreted by some critics as an indication that he had abandoned his socialist beliefs: this was not his intention.)

The tone of the book is on the whole benevolent; it is a *good natured* satire, free of rancour or invective. Ridicule and sarcasm are certainly present, but the story is told with such . detachment and humour that the serious intention underlying the work tends to be masked. Nevertheless there are a number of crucial points when the affectionate tone is deliberately and abruptly changed. One such moment occurs at the conclusion of the scene in which the pigs, hens and sheep confess to crimes instigated by Snowball:

> And so the tale of confessions and executions went on, until there was a pile of corpses lying before Napoleon's feet and the air was heavy with the smell of blood, which had been unknown there since the expulsion of Jones. When it was all

over, the remaining animals, except for the pigs and dogs, crept away in a body. They were shaken and miserable. They did not know which was more shocking—the treachery of the animals who had leagued themselves with Snowball, or the cruel retribution they had just witnessed.

This horrifying scene, the beginning of the reign of terror initiated by Napoleon (and corresponding to the Stalin purge trials) marks a departure from all that has preceded it. Although there has been violence before, most notably in the Battle of the Cowshed, this has been of a faintly comic character—e.g., 'All the pigeons, to the number of thirty-five, flew to and fro over the men's heads and muted upon them from mid-air; and while the men were dealing with this, the geese, who had been hiding behind the hedge, rushed out and pecked viciously at the calves of their legs'. Even during the Battle no one is killed: a stable-lad who is struck on the head by Boxer's iron-shod hoofs is thought to be dead but turns out to be only stunned. The confession of the animals in Chapter 7 is of a very different character. Orwell clearly intends his readers to share his deep sense of revulsion at the treachery and ruthlessness of Napoleon; this revulsion is signalled not merely by a change of style but by a significant transformation of *language*. Hence the sudden transition from the composed, even tone of the first six chapters to the emotive, painful atmosphere of the confession scene. Phrases such as 'the tale of confessions and executions', 'pile of corpses', 'the smell of blood', 'cruel retribution' are clustered together in a single paragraph of great emotional power. When we learn that the animals were 'shaken and miserable' and that they 'huddled about Clover, not speaking', it is possible to share something of their horror and unease at the savagery of Napoleon's punishment and their unspoken awareness that the ideals with which the revolution began have been betrayed. As Clover reflects on these things the reader identifies fully with her unhappiness:

As Clover looked down the hillside her eyes filled with tears. If she could have spoken her thoughts, it would have been to say that this was not what they had aimed at when they had set themselves years ago to work for the overthrow of the human race. These scenes of terror and slaughter were not what they had looked forward to on that night when old Major first stirred them to rebellion. If she herself had had any picture of the future, it had been of a society of animals set free from hunger and the whip, all equal, each working according to his capacity, the strong protecting the weak, as she had protected the lost brood of ducklings with her foreleg on the night of Major's speech.

In passages such as this Orwell demonstrates his mastery of the beast fable as a literary genre. The horse is a dumb animal and cannot therefore express its thoughts in words: this adds appreciably to the pathos of the scene. Clover, however, is not merely an anonymous horse but is an individual with a personality of her own; the homely detail 'as she had protected the lost brood of ducklings with her foreleg' underlines her essential kindliness and motherly instincts. The phrase 'her eyes filled with tears' has an irresistible appeal, imbuing her with human characteristics of sorrow and tenderness. These two passages taken in conjunction—the confession and execution of the alleged traitors, followed by the sadness and disquiet of the remaining animals—surely represent one of the most crucial sequences in the story. In writing these paragraphs Orwell exhibits once again those qualities which transcend journalism and which have ensured a place for *Animal Farm* as one of the most potent myths of our time: the ability to use language in such a way that the reading of a particular passage becomes both an emotional and a literary experience; the alteration of style and tone to indicate a crucial shift of key; the power of entering into the personality of his creations and participating imaginatively in their responses; the gift of communicating complex human feelings in prose of the utmost simplicity and precision.

A Deftly Shaped Satire

'*Animal Farm*,' wrote Orwell, 'was the first book in which I tried, with full consciousness of what I was doing, to fuse political purpose and artistic purpose into one whole.' It is widely regarded as one of his finest works and seems destined to earn for him a posthumous reputation far exceeding any renown he enjoyed during his lifetime. It has taken its place alongside [Voltaire's] *Candide* and the talking horses of [Jonathan Swift's] *Gulliver's Travels* as one of those parables which embody permanent truths: a myth that will long outlast the particular historical events which form its background. Now that it is possible to view the work in context, freed of the emotional circumstances surrounding its publication, we can recognise it for what it is: a dystopia, a satirical commentary upon human societies which vividly recalls Swift's *A Tale of a Tub*.

It is unique among Orwell's full-length works in that he himself as narrator or *alter ego* is absent. Elsewhere he is either the narrator in a story told in the first person (e.g., *Down and Out in Paris and London*) or one of the principal characters (for example, Gordon Comstock in *Keep the Aspidistra Flying*) or is present in the sense that he comments upon the thoughts and behaviour of his protagonists. *Animal Farm*, however, is written throughout in a plain, dispassionate, almost neutral style which admirably suits its theme and in which his distinctive voice is not felt. The result is a gain in impersonality which strengthens the satirical elements in the work and at the same time enhances its ability to stimulate thought and disturb the emotions. Orwell as commentator and interpreter is missing; as a shaping presence, organising and fashioning his material, he is there. It is this which gives the book its distinctive flavour: it is 'Orwellian' in the sense that it deals with themes characteristic of its author and in language of the utmost simplicity; only he could have written it. Yet the 'I' of the previous works, the idiosyncratic presence who combined passionate socialist beliefs with a desire to conserve the past, remains outside the frame he has created.

Animal Farm Remains Relevant

The essential thesis of the book, then, is that all human revolutions fail to achieve the lofty expectations of their originators; that with the passage of time the ideals and precepts which inspired the revolution become more and more diluted; that revolutions, whilst professing democracy and equality, tend to produce a ruling élite which concentrates power in its own hands; that the blame for the failure of policies is placed firmly on external factors and not on internal leadership; that the ruling élite becomes corrupted by the growth of its own power until at last it is responsible to no one but itself and ruthlessly destroys any opposition. Tyranny is by definition evil, regardless of its political complexion.

Seen in these terms *Animal Farm* has a relevance to twentieth-century history far wider than a strictly literal interpretation would suggest. Indeed, the satire continues to have relevance despite the fact that the events which inspired it are now a matter of history. One of the reasons why the book has such a wide appeal today is that it possesses those timeless qualities which enable readers of different generations and different cultures to apply its lessons to their own circumstances. One commentator has shrewdly observed: 'There have been, are, and always will be pigs in every society, Orwell states, and they will always grab power. Even more cruel is the conclusion that *everyone* in the society, wittingly or unwittingly, contributes to the pigs' tyranny.' The book is then a profoundly pessimistic fable, a parable which owes its origins to the betrayed idealism of *Homage to Catalonia* and which anticipates the hopelessness and regimentation of *Nineteen Eighty-Four*.

Animal Farm Satirizes the Failure of Revolutions and Expresses an Ideal of Human Decency

Averil Gardner

Author and literary critic Averil Gardner taught at the Memorial University of Newfoundland in Canada.

Orwell was passionate about human liberty and was an animal lover. In the following selection, Averil Gardner describes how Orwell infused his political message with emotional impact through his skillful depiction of the animals in Animal Farm. *In his seemingly simple story about animals, Gardner asserts, Orwell has written a book that attacks the Soviet Union for its failure to live up to its revolutionary ideals at the same time that it presents a universal message about the human flaw that causes all revolutions to fail—the abuse of power.*

According to the varying predispositions of readers, argument may arise as to whether *Animal Farm* focuses essentially on the failure of the Russian revolution, or on the inherent likelihood of all revolutions to fail. Related to this may be uncertainty about whether the book points to particular historical causes for failure, the abuse of power by a particular class in particular circumstances, for instance; or to ineradicable flaws in human nature—the "darkness of man's heart" later explored by William Golding in *Lord of the Flies* (1954)—that may doom any society to less than perfection. Orwell's own intellectual view on the first matter, expressed in his essay on Arthur Koestler, was that "all revolutions are failures but

Averil Gardner, "*Animal Farm,*" *George Orwell,* New York, NY: Twayne Publishers, 1995, pp. 96–107. Copyright © 1995 by Simon & Schuster Macmillan. Reproduced by permission of Gale, a part of Cengage Learning.

they are not all the same failure"; and yet, though his story allegorizes Russia, the fact that its protagonists are "beasts of England" on an English farm is bound to pull against that external frame of reference. In the second matter, all one can say is that Orwell's agnostic humanism would probably have obliged him to reject the Christian pessimism of Golding, but that the residual Anglicanism that caused him to wish to be buried in a country churchyard would surely have enabled him to understand it. The idea, in Orwell's last book [*Nineteen Eighty-Four*], of the future as "a boot stamping on a human face—for ever" seems at least as grounded in theological doctrines of innate depravity as in political second sight, and at the conclusion of *Animal Farm* one's sense of the human-faced, whip-carrying pigs as objects of the author's satire is outweighed by one's despairing pity for the animals looking on, and locked apparently forever into the brave new world to which the pigs' descent into "humanness" has brought them.

A Haunting Intensity

It is hard to understand how *Animal Farm* could ever have been described, as it was in the Penguin Books blurb a year after Orwell's death, as "a good-natured satire on dictatorship." Whatever specifics Orwell meant to express, the haunting allegory in which he expressed them certainly "means more" as an autonomous creation, if only because in espousing the simplicity of language proper to a story about animals, he also unlocked a deeper level of emotional response than could have been reached by a detailed historical treatment of revolution. Paradoxically, the animal fable afforded Orwell a powerful vehicle in which to express his ideal of "human decency." Embodied in a human story, where complexities of character and motive must be treated, "decency" can seem as a political notion naive and sentimental; but for animals to attempt to attain a society based on it seems appropriate. When they fail, or are frustrated, in their attempt, what is evoked in the reader is more than regret: it is a naked sorrow at defenselessness. In chapter 9, when Boxer the cart-horse is carried off in the knacker's [a person who buys old horses for slaughter] van, Orwell fuses allegory—the betrayed proletariat—so perfectly with story—a real horse treated with cruel ingratitude—that the nature of most readers' feelings must be as impossible to analyze as it is easy to imagine.

Reviewing *Animal Farm* in *Horizon*, Cyril Connolly expressed its mixture of elements by calling it "a fairy story told by a great lover of liberty and a great lover of animals." Its moral and satiric thrust derive straightforwardly enough from the former aspect of Orwell. But much of the emotional power of the book is produced by its use for allegorical purposes of realistic animals, whose presentation Orwell could count on to tap a deep vein of protective sentiment in British readers. It is tempting to scholars and critics to adduce literary or folkloric sources for this responsiveness to animals in the works of Aesop and [Jean] La Fontaine, but, though Orwell no doubt shared with some of his readers a knowledge of such writings, it seems probable that his, and their, feeling for animals had less "highbrow" origins: in nursery rhymes featuring animals, in the farm animal toys played with by children of Orwell's generation, and in such a children's book as Anna Sewell's *Black Beauty* (1877), which combined a realistic and unsentimental picture of the lives of various types or horses with a high-minded Victorian inculcation of the need for kindness to animals. Given Orwell's admiration for such "Victorian" classics as [Harriet Beecher Stowe's] *Uncle Tom's Cabin* and [Louisa May Alcott's] *Little Women*, it does not seem too farfetched to suppose that the simple clarity of *Black Beauty* may have provided him with a model of style, just as [Jonathan] Swift's *Gulliver's Travels* and *A Tale of a Tub* are generally agreed to have influenced his allegorical approach.

Orwell was a "lover of animals" this side of idolatry, and his realistic presentation of them is as notable as their potential to involve the reader's emotions. It was from life more than from literature that Orwell drew his knowledge of animals, in common with those of his readers who had, or have, experienced farms either through a rural upbringing, through seeing animals in fields on trips into the country, or, in wartime Britain, as a result of evacuation in childhood from towns likely to be bombed to safe, though at first strange, agricultural areas. Like many children, Orwell had kept pets; in England he had shot rabbits (admitted as "comrades" in *Animal Farm*), in Burma pigeons, as well as the solitary elephant whose death he so movingly described in "Shooting an Elephant." Though he never ran a farm himself, the village where he lived from 1936 to 1940 was in farming country, and there he kept hens, a goat (whose name, Muriel, he used for the goat in *Animal Farm*), and a dog. His name for that dog, Marx, may have sparked Orwell's brilliantly simple notion of an entire farm—a society of animals controlled by humans—as an allegory first for capitalism, then for communism, which he calls "Animalism." It is surely no accident that the only place name that occurs in *Animal Farm*, the nearby small town of "Willingdon," closely resembles the name of Orwell's Hertfordshire village, Wallington.

That resemblance may explain the particular poignancy one recognizes in Orwell's occasional brief passages of landscape description in *Animal Farm*, that near the end of chapter 7 being the most lyrical. The revolution fails, but the place in which it fails reflected Orwell's memory of a country life that, for all its relative poverty, he had enjoyed and had associated with the last years of peace. But there is another, more sinister echo in Orwell's fictional location, which comes from further back and which, of all *Animal Farm*'s readers in 1945, perhaps only Cyril Connolly would have recognized: only three miles from Orwell's hated preparatory school, St. Cyprian's, lay the small Sussex village of Willingdon, on the other side of a downland hill of that name, which he could have looked toward from Eastbourne. Perhaps at least some of the unhappiness conveyed in *Animal Farm*, as well as some or its satire, flows out of memories of that oppressive system. Minimus's "Animal Farm" jingle in chapter 7, and the groveling poem to Napoleon in chapter 8, have the doggerel banality of English "school songs," and *Minimus* itself is the Latin term once used in school roll calls to distinguish the youngest of three attending siblings, the oldest, of course, being *Major*, like the prize old boar whose doctrines are so amended and reduced as the revolution goes on. Were "Sambo" and "Flip" the original autocratic pigs of Orwell's imaginative experience? He certainly had no love for real pigs, which is not the universal reaction. They are chosen to represent rulers in *Animal Farm* because of their intelligence, but also because of their greed and their cunning. When Orwell "tried the experiment of keeping a pig" on [the Hebridean island of] Jura in 1948, he found it "destructive and greedy," and displayed in his letters on the subject a dislike that verges on the vindictive: "They really are disgusting brutes and we are all longing for the day when he goes to the butcher."

All of these various elements—external political reality, the complex of emotions evoked by animals, the throb of authorial memories—contribute a peculiar, often foreboding, intensity to Orwell's narrative, creating around it a penumbra of connotation. Orwell's subtitle, "A Fairy Story," may have been intended not only as an ironic comment on the book's historical relevance but also as an accurate indication of its poetic quality. But to say this is not to reduce the centrality of *Animal Farm*'s story line, which is admirably simple—crisp and grave by turns—in style, evenly paced, marked by rich inventiveness of phrase and incident, and skilled in offsetting the inevitability of its overall development by means of local suspense and surprises. Orwell's narrative clarity in *Animal Farm* may have owed something to his having obtained before publication the reaction of an attentive and intelligent reader:

though he had never done so before with anyone else, Orwell discussed the book "in considerable detail" with his wife, Eileen, and told a friend she had helped in its planning.

Boiling Down Political History to Essentials

The use of the animal fable assisted Orwell not only with the atmosphere of his story, but with its scope and structure, enabling him both to boil down the complex details of political history to their essentials and to telescope them into memorable brevity. The Russian events, which took twenty-six years to unfold, from the anticapitalist revolution of 1917 to the rapprochement with capitalism in November 1943 (when [Joseph] Stalin met with [Franklin Delano] Roosevelt and [Winston] Churchill at the Teheran conference) are compressed in *Animal Farm* into ten short chapters covering nine or ten years, a credible equivalent in animal terms. The illicit night meeting with which the novel opens, at which the "wise and benevolent" old boar Major ([Karl] Marx/ [Vladimir] Lenin) describes the exploitation of animals by humans and forecasts "a golden future time" of a world without humans, establishes the Soviet political allegory immediately by its statement that "all animals are comrades," while its other slogan, "all animals are equal," allows a wider reading, applicable alike to Jeffersonian idealism and British democratic socialism. Thus the abrupt abolition in chapter 7 of the stirring song "Beasts of England," an animal version of [poet William] Blake's "Jerusalem," can be seen not only as a symbol of the decay of communist notions of a perfect state, but also, since at the end it is the once dreaded human beings the pig-rulers come to resemble, as Orwell's more general comment on the decline of true liberty and equality in the West.

The progress of the revolution from a common idealism to a two-tier, and later a three-tier, state system of leader, police, workers, takes only five chapters. Even before the drunken Mr. Jones is ousted by a spontaneous uprising sparked by hunger, and the feudally named "Manor Farm" becomes the egalitarian "Animal Farm" with its seven simple commandments and its green and white version of the Russian hammer and sickle flag, the pigs have emerged as natural organizers. When the hay harvest is gathered in (chap. 3), it is the other animals, particularly the two cart-horses, Boxer and Clover, who do the work while the clever pigs, led by the strong, silent Napoleon (Stalin) and the intellectually innovative Snowball (Trotsky), not only supervise but keep for themselves all milk and apples on the grounds that they are good for the brain. For Orwell, the manipulative speech by which the propagandist porker, Squealer, justifies this to the other animals was the key passage of *Animal Farm*: it demonstrates both the greed and the hypocrisy involved in the urge to power, which disguises itself as sacrifice for the common good. At first, the reader shares in the euphoria and pride of the animals in their early period of success and freedom from obvious oppression. When this reaches its climax in the triumphant, mock-heroic "Battle of the Cowshed" (chap. 4), the reader can admire alike the strength of Boxer and the courage and strategic skill of Snowball, both of whom are awarded the newly created order "Animal Hero, First Class." But there are ominous undercurrents even here. The decent Boxer, thinking he has killed a stable lad, is sorry; for Snowball the death does not matter. In this divergence is visible the gap that gradually widens between the pigs—who first put forward all the resolutions at the democratic Sunday meetings (chap. 3) and then take over all policy decisions on the farm (chap. 4)—and the rank-and-file animal workers, who accept direction with naive optimism.

The distinction between rulers and ruled is given more brutal form in chapter 5, at the end of only the first year of the revolution, when the constant disagreement between Napoleon and Snowball on matters of policy comes to a head. In foreign policy, represented by Animal Farm's relationship with its human-run neighbors, Foxwood and Pinchfield, Napoleon favors a defensive buildup of armaments, Snowball an attempt at destabilization by propaganda. Domestically, Napoleon urges increased food production, Snowball the building of a windmill that, when finished, will reduce working hours. When Snowball's eloquence threatens to win the day, Napoleon suddenly calls up a pack of fierce dogs who chase Snowball off the farm—a simplified reenactment of Trotsky's expulsion from Russia in 1929. Henceforth the leader principle replaces democracy: reared up from puppies in secret, the dogs are as exclusively loyal to Napoleon as their predecessors had been to Mr. Jones. "Meetings" are immediately abolished, being replaced by weekly "Orders" drawn up by Napoleon and a select politburo of pigs. Animal Farm is now run by a mixture of intimidation and chicanery, the dogs of the KGB [the Soviet Union's security and intelligence agency] ever ready to growl down dissent, Squealer always on hand to extol Napoleon, any failure in whose selfless vigilance, the other animals are persuaded, will result in the return of the hated Jones.

Chapters 6 through 9, covering three more years, chart a progressive and irreversible decline, which is shown in three main ways, all interrelated and amounting to a bitter gloss on the phrase that opens chapter 6: "All that year the animals worked like slaves." The "like" is seen as more and more superfluous: the animals *are* slaves, to their own noble idealism, to the regime that dupes and mistreats them, and to the loss of memory the regime's rewriting of history brings about. Napoleon first appropriates Snowball's plans for a windmill, which in Soviet terms represent industrialization, then claims Snowball stole them from him; similarly, Snowball's role in the Battle of the Cowshed is bit by bit downgraded until at last he is represented as having led the opposing, human forces. Like Trotsky, Snowball is turned into the arch-criminal and convenient bogy, and in chapter 7, a grimly vivid miniature of the Soviet purges of the 1930s, a number of animals, including four porkers, and some hens who have opposed Napoleon's collectivization, are seized and executed after confessing they have been in league with Snowball. The event leaves the other animals "shaken and miserable," but as much over the "treachery" they credit as over the "cruel retribution" they have witnessed. Yet loyalty, obedience and discipline, the watchwords of Animal Farm since chapter 5, do not guarantee gratitude. When Boxer, whose personal slogans are "I will work harder" and "Napoleon is always right," collapses under a load of stone for the windmill, he is cheated of the promised retirement he has earned. Instead, he is carted off to the knacker's (chap.9), to a death that, in effect, turns him into food for dogs and "another case of whisky for the pigs." Though at the time the other animals utter "a cry of horror" and try to warn him, they are all too easily convinced by Squealer later that "our leader, Comrade Napoleon" could not possibly have let such a thing happen.

The blurring of the past and the hardening shape of the present, grim, greedy, or just pragmatic, are accompanied by a betrayal of the spirit of the revolution exemplified in the amendments made to its letter, the "seven commandments" of "Animalism" promulgated in chapter 2. Constantly these are changed, just before the puzzled animals can check their uneasy memories against them, to keep pace with the increasing decadence and authoritarianism of the pigs. Hence in turn. "No animal shall sleep in a bed" becomes, when the pigs move into the farmhouse in chapter 6, "No animal shall sleep in a bed with sheets," and after the savage killings in chapter 7, "No animal shall kill any other animal" is modified by the addition of "without cause."

A Universal Notion of Liberty

This insidious process of formal tinkering reaches its brilliant, and depressing, climax at the end of the book. More and more the pigs have gravitated toward the human world, first

Animal Farm poster. The lettering hints at the Cyrillic alphabet, used in the Russian language. The handwritten note summarizes two commandments of the revolution that were betrayed and eventually failed completely. © Peter Coombs/Alamy.

through trade and alliances (the selling of timber to Mr. Frederick of Pinchfield is the animal equivalent of the short-lived

Nazi-Soviet nonaggression pact of 1939); then, as they cel-
ebrate their Pyrrhic victory over him at "the Battle of the
Windmill" (chap. 8), through drinking alcohol. More and
more has Napoleon, "elected" president in chapter 9, become
the remote object of a personality cult in a system marked by
"re-adjustment" of rations for workers and the empty "dignity" of "more songs, more speeches, more processions." The
two trends meet and fuse in chapter 10, set a few years later
on in a world where almost none remembers either "the old
days before the Rebellion" or the period of freedom immediately after it. Prosperity has come, but only to the pigs and the
dogs; for the rest "life was as it had always been." Despite this,
the animals still retain hope for the earthly millennium when
"the green fields of England should be untrodden by human
feet," still hum the proscribed "Beasts of England" in secret,
and still take pride in the fact that "they were not as other
animals. If they were hungry, it was not from feeding tyrannical human beings; if they worked hard, at least they worked
for themselves. No creature among them went upon two legs.
No creature called any other creature 'Master'. All animals
were equal."

The paragraph from which this passage comes is among
the most eloquent pieces of writing in all Orwell's work. It is a
statement that, though it sits well with the particular Soviet
allegory of *Animal Farm* also rises strongly out of it to present
a universal notion of liberty. For Orwell, it is the proletariat,
rather than the politicians or the intelligentsia, who keep the
flame of idealism alive. Yet, in the context Orwell has built up,
the belief is no more than a pathetic dream, and its last phrase
is like a tree waiting for the axe. The axe falls almost immediately. Squealer, then the other pigs, then Napoleon, emerge
from the farmhouse walking on two legs; the latter carries a
whip, the hated symbol of human beings, in his trotter. The
mob of sheep, whose chant used to be "Four legs good, two
legs bad," have been coached to chant "Four legs good, two

legs *better*," the identical verbal pattern expressing a completely opposite meaning. Yet this *has* a meaning, however horrifying in the context. The ultimate verbal expression of tyranny is linguistic nonsense, and on the wall of the barn the one remaining commandment is Orwell's magnificent and unforgettable example of it: "All animals are equal, but some animals are more equal than others." The reader's amusement at the cleverness of this [Oscar] Wildean trope is quickly smothered under the weight of the facts and events it implies. The final animal-human banquet, Orwell's version of the Teheran conference, drives home the stark contrast between hope and reality, as Mr. Pilkington, the capitalist West, praises the "discipline and orderliness" of Animal Farm, and utters the bon mot that widens the book to more than an anti-Communist allegory: "If you have your lower animals to contend with . . . we have our lower classes." With the announced change of name back to "Manor Farm," the revolution has come full circle, and however the two groups, pigs and humans, may quarrel, they look the same to the animals gazing in, the working classes who, it seems, are betrayed by all governments.

Maintaining Liberty Takes Vigilance

One draws that last inference uneasily. Had Orwell gone ahead in 1944 and brought out *Animal Farm* at his own expense, he intended to preface it with an essay containing this sentence: "If liberty means anything at all it means the right to tell people what they do not wish to hear." His anxiety to show the Soviet system in its true colors—how after its pretensions to a greater liberty, it merely approximated capitalism and reintroduced hierarchy in a new guise—causes his allegorical method to imply stronger criticism of the Western allies, and of Roosevelt and Churchill, than one can believe he fully intended. Nevertheless, the eagerness of Mr. Pilkington and his neighbors to "introduce on their own farms" the harsher regime of the pigs strikes a sinister note, and reflects the fear shown in many of Orwell's essays that liberty would diminish everywhere if vigilance relaxed.

Good allegories, as William Empson told Orwell in 1945, are apt to mean "more than their authors mean"; allegories may also mean things the author does not mean. Allegory distorts as well as simplifies, as critics, including Orwell himself, have felt about book 4 of *Gulliver's Travels*. On the whole, the allegory of *Animal Farm* works well enough in terms of Orwell's topical intention, to discredit the Soviet system by showing its inhumanity and its back-sliding from ideals Orwell valued and still hoped could be achieved. The Swiftian element in the book lies only partly in the doubts it casts on that hope; it lies also in its rich fictional inventiveness, the scores of small details—the burial of the hams in chapter 2, the "reverent" filing past Major's skull in chapter 5, the ribbons of Mollie and the ribbons of the pigs—by which allegorical purpose is given a local habitation in a sharply visualized community of animals.

It is this sharpness of visualization and the emotional resonance it creates that have ensured *Animal Farm* what seems likely to be a permanent place in literature. Mixing, as Bernard Crick has well expressed it, "serenity of tone" and "bitterness of content," it is neither simple allegory nor simple animal fable. Graham Greene rightly noted in his review that we "become involved in the fate" of the animals. We care about them too much merely to translate events into their historical equivalent. Reading the fables of Aesop and La Fontaine, we are sufficiently distant to be able to laugh at the dupe as well as to reprimand the trickster. There is no such possibility in *Animal Farm*, nor, by the end, can we escape the weight of the book's sadness by thinking that these things have only happened to animals. We took from the oppressed animals in the book to the oppressed human beings outside and back again, and can see no difference.

Animal Farm Is Artistically Satisfying but Ambiguous

Robert Pearce

Robert Pearce, an historian and educator, taught at the University of Cumbria in Lancaster, England, before becoming a full-time author.

In the following selection, Robert Pearce contends that George Orwell's intent in Animal Farm *was to describe the failure of the Russian Revolution rather than to say that all revolutions are doomed to failure. However, Pearce finds that Orwell's purpose is obscured by several aspects of the book that are not analogous to events in Russia. For instance, there is no equivalent to Vladimir Lenin in* Animal Farm, *and World War I is omitted. Despite the ambiguity of the text, Pearce states,* Animal Farm *is a brilliant, if flawed, success.*

The key to the success of *Animal Farm* lies in the fact that it was not just a political novel. Nor was Orwell the politics-obsessed figure of legend. His childhood friend Cyril Connolly wrote that he was always incorrigibly political, so that he couldn't blow his nose without moralizing on the state of the linen industry. Yet such a view is partly exaggeration, partly anachronism. Orwell himself, in a poem of 1936, insisted that he 'wasn't born for an age like this', the era of mass propaganda, the bomber and rubber truncheons [nightsticks]. Indeed even at his most politically committed he took delight in a Woolworth's rose ('ten years of pleasure for sixpence'), in seeing a kestrel flying over the Deptford gasworks and in hearing a 'first-rate performance by a blackbird in the Euston Road'. He was able to glory in the spring and to praise the

Robert Pearce, "*Animal Farm*: Sixty Years On," *History Today*, vol. 55, no. 8, August 2005, pp. 47–53. Copyright © 2005 History Today Ltd. Reproduced by permission.

common toad, whose eye was the most beautiful of any living creature's. The really important things in life, Orwell implied, are private not political. Man stayed human only by preserving 'large patches of simplicity in his life'. Most important of all was the need for something to believe in, despite the decay of traditional religious belief, for 'man cannot live by hedonism alone'.

> So long as I remain alive and well I shall continue to feel strongly about prose style, to love the surface of the earth, and to take pleasure in solid objects and scraps of useless information . . .

Well Written with a Gentle Humour

Such non-political concerns undoubtedly contributed to *Animal Farm*'s success. The book contains some of Orwell's finest writing. [Publisher Frederic] Warburg considered it a 'prose poem' written 'almost effortlessly'. He was wrong about the effort. Orwell admitted that it was the only one of his books 'I really sweated over'. It was also the only one he received help with, his wife Eileen commenting on the extracts he read to her every night. Generally a severe critic of his own work, Orwell was nevertheless pleased with the aesthetic aspects of *Animal Farm*. He castigated its reviewers as 'grudging swine . . . not one of them said it's a beautiful book'. After many hard years of apprenticeship, he was now producing his ideal of window-pane prose. (Over-diligent critics have deplored that he used 'said' thirty-four times, out of sixty-four 'verbs of saying', but the simple word repeated only added to the mythic, fairy-tale quality Orwell was attempting to create.)

The book's gentle humour also contributed to its popularity. After the revolution, 'some hams hanging in the kitchen were taken out for burial', the book's most celebrated joke; but there are many others. Several commentators attribute this quality to Eileen's influence, but in fact humour had been a conspicuous part of Orwell's writing from earliest days, the obverse of his famous pessimism. Similarly, the book gained enormously from his expertise as a countryman. He had long equated the countryside with decency, and his knowledge of things rural went back to his childhood and to the joy of his initiation into natural history by R.L. Sillar at St Cyprian's prep school in Eastbourne. The result is that the routines of farming in the book are convincing—from the 'pop-holes' of the first sentence, to Old Major's uncut tushes, the Number 6 shot in Jones's gun, the potatoes that 'frosted in the clamps' and the coccidiosis from which hens were said to have died.

Adding authenticity is Orwell's knowledge of animals. Most of the good memories of his childhood, he once wrote, were in some way connected with animals. In Burma in the 1920s he recruited a motley collection of strays, and at Wallington from 1936 he kept a goat called Muriel. As a man, he had an acute eye for cruelty towards animals, though his sympathy stopped well short of vegetarianism. He could hardly look at the hindquarters of a gazelle 'without thinking of mint sauce'. Pigs, on the other hand, he told David Astor, 'are most annoying destructive animals . . . They are hard to keep out of anywhere because they are so strong and cunning.'

Orwell had for some time been describing human beings as animals. A good example is his description of Lord Beaverbrook, who looked 'more like a monkey on a stick than you would think possible for anyone who was not doing it on purpose'. Hence role-reversal—endowing animals with human characteristics—must have seemed perfectly normal, especially to one so well read in beast-fables, beginning with Beatrix Potter's Pigling Bland, which he read twice to childhood friend Jacintha Buddicom and whose frontispiece showed two pigs walking on their hind legs.

Animal Farm Expresses Political Passion

Yet when all is said and done, political passion lies at the heart of *Animal Farm*. When Orwell lacked a political purpose, he wrote in 1946, he produced 'lifeless books and was betrayed into purple passages, sentences without meaning, decorative adjectives and humbug generally'. His aim was to expose the 'Soviet myth' for British readers.

When he returned from Burma in 1927 Orwell may be described as leftwing, and [historian and critic] John Newsinger believes he was soon flirting with Communism. Nevertheless he had no faith in Marxist theory: using Marxism to analyse the English class system, he once wrote, was rather like attempting to carve a duck with a chopper. In 1936, in *The Road to Wigan Pier*, he commended socialism because it equated with 'justice and common decency', but he referred scathingly to 'the stupid cult of Russia'. On Christmas Day 1936 he left Britain to fight for the republican side in the Spanish civil war, as part of an Independent Labour Party contingent which served with the anarchist POUM militia. The effects of this were to heighten his beliefs. Having seen a classless society in Barcelona, he now believed in socialism more than ever before. But after witnessing the Soviet attempt to destroy the social revolution in Spain, and rivet fascism on the Spanish workers under the pretext of resisting fascism, he became adamantly anti-Stalinist [Joseph Stalin was the Soviet leader]. The main sin of the Left in Britain, he insisted, was that while it was anti-fascist it was not anti-totalitarian. For a time during the Second World War, Orwell considered it necessary to praise Stalin ('I never thought I should live to say "Good luck to Comrade Stalin" but I do'), but by November 1943 he decided it was time to bury him. He would say exactly what he thought about the betrayal of the Russian revolution in order to help revivify a realistic democratic socialist movement at home.

Problematic Parallels

Many parallels between Russian history and the revolution at Manor Farm are unmistakable. Clearly Old Major represents [Karl] Marx, Napoleon is Stalin, Snowball is [Leon] Trotsky,

Pilkington is Britain, Frederick Germany, the dogs are the OGPU/NKVD [Soviet police and security forces]. The battle of the cowshed represents the Allied invasion of 1918, the battle of the windmill is the Nazi invasion of 1941, while the windmill itself represents the Five Year Plans. Orwell had merely changed the chronological order of events, to meet the needs of symmetry of plot. There are far more parallels than most readers realise, and another score [twenty] could be specified. When in chapter eight Orwell wrote that, during the battle of the windmill, 'all the animals, except Napoleon, flung themselves flat on their bellies' he had changed an earlier proof version ('all the animals including Napoleon') because he had received reliable information, from Joseph Czapaski, ironically a Polish survivor of the Gulag [Soviet forced labor camps], that Stalin bravely stayed in Moscow during the German advance.

Yet, in fact, the parallels are problematical. Some commentators have judged that [Vladimir] Lenin was part of the Old Major character, some that he was part of Napoleon or Snowball, but in reality Lenin was omitted. Orwell believed that Lenin 'would have come to resemble Stalin if he had happened to survive' (though he changed his mind later), and therefore was a disposable figure. But this renders *Animal Farm* almost *Hamlet* without the prince. Nor is there an equivalent of the First World War in the book. Farmer Jones does not suffer a catastrophe that shook Manor Farm to its foundations, he simply gets drunk once too often. Also, many of Orwell's details have been misunderstood. It has been suggested that Napoleon's upright stance at the battle of the windmill probably indicated collusion with the invaders. Snowball's insistence on literacy classes has been taken to indicate that Orwell was a Trotskyite, which he expressly denied. Squealer has been wrongly identified with Vladimir Mayakovsky, the Stalinist versifier who in fact is represented by Minimus in the book. So who is Squealer? There was certainly no equivalent in Soviet history—and anyone as prominent and powerful would surely not have survived the purges. (Was he *Pravda* [the Communist Party newspaper] personified? Or perhaps he was based on Dr. [Joseph] Goebbels [the Nazi minister of propaganda]?) The re-admission of Moses to *Animal Farm* has been said to represent Stalin's meeting with U.S. parish priest Father Stanislaw Orlemanski, though this took place on April 28th, 1944, several months after Orwell had finished the book. Similarly, the final scene is sometimes anachronistically equated with the Yalta rather than the Teheran conference.

Most difficult of all is the issue of whether in *Animal Farm* Orwell was explaining why one particular revolution failed or implying that all revolutions fail. There is no didactic voice, and therefore there is room for doubt. Does any author, *pace* ["in peace"; i.e., no offense to] Orwell, ever have 'full consciousness of what he is doing'? Reading—even of Orwell's pellucid prose—is a sort of rewriting, and no authors have control over what others make of their works.

There is little reason to suppose that Orwell was critical of Old Major's call for revolution (though some claim that he was, pointing to rhetorical ploys and an authoritarian edge in his speech). Certainly there is no reason to doubt Orwell's praise of the immediate post-revolution period, when 'everyone worked according to his capacity', no one stole and the animals were 'happy as they had never conceived it possible to be'. This was a period of true socialism, paralleled by the 'wonderful things' Orwell had observed in Barcelona. But what went wrong? Was the tyranny of the pigs inevitable? What exactly was the moral of *Animal Farm*?

Orwell explained in 1946 that he intended the book:

primarily as a satire on the Russian revolution. But I did mean it to have a wider application in so much as I meant that that kind of revolution (violent conspiratorial revolution, led by unconsciously power-hungry people) can only lead to a change of masters. I meant the moral to be that revolutions only effect a radical improvement when the masses are alert and know how to chuck out their leaders as soon as the latter have done their job. The turning point of the story was supposed to be when the pigs kept the milk and apples for themselves ... If the other animals had had the sense to put their foot down, it would have been all right.

The problem here is simply that Orwell had to spell out the moral, for, as he wrote in the introduction to the Ukrainian edition, if the book 'does not speak for itself, it is a failure'. The overwhelming majority of readers carry away from *Animal Farm* the conviction that the animals, except the pigs, are innocent dupes. The corruption of the revolution is so gradual and insidious that it seems inevitable. In particular Boxer, the Stakhanovite [diligent and productive] carthorse, is universally regarded as the book's hero, a character whose pathos has led him to be seen as an equine Little Nell. Are we supposed to condemn him for failing to stand up to Napoleon? The fact is that he simply does not have the brains to do so. Orwell pointed to his unintelligence many times, and even gave him a 'somewhat stupid appearance'. In the play he adapted from the book, broadcast in January 1947, Orwell made this prosaically clear. 'I am not good at thinking things out for myself,' states the hapless Boxer; 'The pigs are cleverest ... My brain is not good.' If the intellectually inferior animals were supposed to control the self-evidently superior pigs, then surely there was no hope for a successful socialist revolution.

Hard-Working but Inferior

When T.S. Eliot read the manuscript of *Animal Farm* for Faber & Faber, he commented that the novel's effect seemed to him 'one of negation'. The pigs were far more intelligent than the other animals and the best qualified to run the farm, so what was really needed 'was not more communism but more public-spirited pigs'. No writer has done other than lambast Eliot's point of view, and with some reason, since Orwell aimed primarily to destroy the myth of the USSR as a socialist country. Yet Orwell had not intended to be entirely negative, and there is logic in Eliot's viewpoint. Since the pigs were the most intelligent animals, and the decent, loyal Boxer could never manage to master more than four letters of the alphabet, then if there was hope it lay with the porkers.

Orwell's description of the worker-animals owed a good deal to his understanding—or misunderstanding—of British workers. He wrote in 1936, very candidly, that he was brought up in the sort of middle-class family that regarded workers as 'almost sub-human'. He added that every middle-class person 'has a dormant class-prejudice'. This seems true of Orwell himself. He often praised the working class for their stoicism and hard work—but never for their intelligence or leadership. To his mind, workers were not just ordinary people whose education had often limited their intellectual horizons, they were inherently mentally inferior. He had never known a working man, he wrote, 'who grasps the deeper implications of socialism', and he habitually depicted the proletariat as passive. 'There is no mob any more,' he said, after spending two months in the north of England in 1936, 'only a flock'. In 1942 he wrote that the English workers were like a plant, 'blind and stupid but it knows enough to keep pushing towards the light'—a doublethink that tells us much about Orwell's ambivalence towards the working class. So does his habit of mocking their pronunciation—their 'romance' and 'sez', though the latter is the dictionary-correct way of pronouncing 'says'.

[Writer and critic] Raymond Williams was incorrect to assert that Orwell was no longer a socialist when he wrote *Animal Farm*. But he was surely right to insist that the book was a simplification, with the faults and virtues that flow therefrom. Orwell undoubtedly hit the Soviet target with his simple farmyard story, but there was collateral damage. It became all too easy for the Right to use his work as propaganda that all revolutions degenerate into despotism.

When Orwell described *Animal Farm* as a 'little squib' he was being self-deprecatory, but he wasn't wholly satisfied with it. In the same paragraph in which he revealed that he'd tried to fuse political and artistic purposes into a whole, he admitted that 'every book is a failure'. He wasn't trying to attack the whole concept of revolution, far from it. But his simple, moving account of revolutionary failure in the USSR contained the flaw that, for many readers, it made all revolutions seem doomed.

No doubt Orwell could have written an unambiguous propagandist pamphlet. Yet we should be grateful that instead he wrote a work of art, something which by its very nature is open to divergent interpretations. *Animal Farm* is a superb but ambiguous satire on a particular revolution. It is also a more general allegory, into which human imagination will continue to breathe life in unexpected ways. In present-day Asia, for instance, *Animal Farm* is considered one of Orwell's 'Burmese books'. In 2001 a serialization by an opposition newspaper in Zimbabwe, the *Daily News*, had illustrations of Napoleon wearing Robert Mugabe's unmistakable black spectacles.

All books are failures, it is true, but not all failures are equal. Some indeed are brilliant if flawed successes, and some little squibs are in fact quite remarkable rockets.

Orwell Preaches Individual Responsibility as a Weapon Against Dictatorship

Katharine Byrne

Katharine Byrne was a widely published essayist who wrote for publications such as the Chicago Daily News, Commonweal, America, *the* Cleveland Plain Dealer, *the* Detroit Free Press, *and the* Chicago Tribune Magazine.

According to Katharine Byrne in the following essay, Animal Farm *retains its relevance today because it is a warning that liberty can be lost unless citizens remain informed and vigilant. Orwell reminds us, Byrne asserts, that power corrupts and it is the duty of the people to keep their governments honest to their ideals.*

Although he was a respected novelist and journalist in England during the '30s and early '40s George Orwell (1903–50) had a hard time getting *Animal Farm* into print. He finished it in 1944 and sent or carried it from one publisher to another, but no one would take it. World War II was in progress. Russia was our ally and Britain's. A book that satirized the betrayal of Russia's revolution by its leaders was regarded, at the very least, as an affront to a friend. Moreover, an American publisher told him you just can't sell an animal story to adults.

Not until the end of the war in 1945 and the customary reshuffling of friends and enemies was a publisher willing to invest enough precious paper to produce 450 copies. These were sold out within weeks. The Queen dispatched an emis-

Katharine Byrne, "Not All Books Are Created Equal: Orwell & His Animals at Fifty," *Commonweal*, vol. 123, no. 10, May 17, 1996, pp. 14–15. Copyright © 1996 Commonweal Publishing Co., Inc. Reproduced by permission of Commonweal Foundation.

sary to her bookseller-by-appointment, but his shelves were bare; an anarchist book shop offered the Queen a complimentary copy. The book has never been out of print since then, read by millions in dozens of languages. Nineteen ninety-six marks its fiftieth anniversary of publication in the United States.

If you were in high school at any time since the 1950s, you probably read *Animal Farm*, a story of the revolt of Farmer Jones's livestock against their brutal, drunken owner. The venerable boar, Old Major, is the philosopher of the revolution. His ringing words to the clandestine assemblage of animals remind them that their lives are "miserable, laborious, and short," with no share in the fruits of their labor. While ascribing all their troubles to "man," his speech ends with the warning: "Above all, no animal must ever tyrannize over his own kind. Weak or strong, clever or simple, we are all brothers. All animals are equal."

The barnyard is roused to revolution. Led by the pigs, the animals rout Jones and take possession; "Jones's Manor" is now called "Animal Farm." Morale is high. Victory is sweet for the liberated animals but also brief. At first they gambol in joy at the prospect of living out their lives in dignity, sharing in the prosperity their labor produces. Each works hard to sustain the revolution.

Repressors Change, but Repression Remains

But then, inexorably, methodically, equality and freedom are stripped away as the pigs, under Napoleon, a ruler as brutal as Jones was, develop a ruling elite that abrogates all privilege to itself at the expense of the "lower" animals. (The wily pigs explain that they really don't like the milk that they refuse to share with the other animals; they drink it only to keep up their strength so that they can pursue the welfare of all.)

Lies and terror now rule "Animal Farm." In the ultimate reversal of Old Major's words, "all animals are created equal, but some animals are more equal than others." One form of repression has been replaced by another. In the end, the wretched animals are looking in the window at an economic summit between Men and Pigs, "Looking from pig to man, and from man to pig they observe that there is no difference between them." . . .

[As] Orwell tells it, the fable ends with all the brave hopes in ruins. Virtue is crushed and wickedness triumphs. What went wrong? Orwell lays out the story and asks us to look at it. He does not moralize. This is what happened, but we know it is not right. We are left morally indignant at the injustice suffered. Are we to believe that this is the inevitable fate of rebellion? Or that other political systems are better than Stalinist [Soviet leader Joseph Stalin's style of] communism?

As to that, Orwell does not uphold the political systems of the West. The men who come to deal with the ruling pigs, Pilkington from capitalist England and Frederick from Nazi Germany, commiserate with the pigs: "You have your lower animals and we have our lower classes." From his earliest years as a policeman for the British Empire in Burma—an "unsuitable career," he called it—Orwell always spoke out against oppressors of the poor and helpless: returning to England he spoke for the rights of tramps, hop-pickers, or coal miners.

A self-defined democratic Socialist, Orwell had a hard time with other members of the Left. An episode in [Saul] Bellow's *Mr. Sammler's Planet* describes the situation succinctly. Addressing a Columbia University seminar, Mr. Sammler is attempting to defend Orwell's position, but he is interrupted by one of the bearded and unwashed students with "Orwell was a counter-revolutionary shit, and you're an old shit too." With this declaration, the meeting is ingloriously ended.

The Right Appropriates Orwell

Maligned by the Left, Orwell has often been appropriated by the Right. In the flurry of interest that coincided with the year

1984, Norman Podhoretz, editor of *Commentary*, claimed that Orwell would, if he had lived, subscribe to the conservative magazine and to the principles of its editor. In fact, *Animal Farm* had earlier entered the canon of required reading in most high schools for some of the wrong reasons, its author would say—and he did say so.

Orwell was distressed to find his *Animal Farm* and *Nineteen Eighty-Four* being used, especially in the United States, as cold-war weapons, purportedly the work of a repentant Communist who saw the light and wanted to warn the world of the inevitable fruits of revolution. When he saw the issue of Henry Luce's *Life* magazine expounding this idea, Orwell insisted that he had not written a book against Stalinism to deny the right of revolt by oppressed people, nor to advance American foreign policy. "My books," he said, "are about the perversions that any centralized economy is liable to."

In a letter to Dwight Macdonald, editor of *Politics*, Orwell further explained, "Revolutions led by power-hungry people can only lead to a change of masters. . . . Revolutions only effect a radical improvement when the masses are alert and know how to chuck out their leaders as soon as the latter have done their job. . . . You can't have a revolution unless you make it for your self; there is no such thing as a benevolent dictatorship."

Animal Farm's Message Still Relevant

Should *Animal Farm* be read during the next fifty years? Of course, but for the right reasons: setting up as it does, with crystal clarity, the price paid when we do not safeguard our freedoms. The hard-working wretches of the world contribute to their own fate in their ignorant loyalty and apathy. In the book, the huge cart-horse, Boxer, a faithful, unquestioning worker ("I will get up earlier; I will work harder . . . Napoleon is always right") is sent to the knackers [horse slaughterers] as soon as his usefulness is over. As he is carried off to his death, the weak protest of his hooves against the side of the van sounds the dying hope of the animals betrayed. The tendency of power to corrupt must always be recognized; people's hold over their own fate must prevail: an alert, informed, and wary electorate.

Is *Animal Farm* out of date since the Soviet Socialist Republics, as constituted, have failed? Only if it is read for the wrong reasons. The tale about independence won but lost continues to remind us that freedom is fragile and precious. Power corrupts, and there are forces at work seeking to wield it.

I have spoken to ten or twelve English teachers, from Highland Park, Illinois, to Highland Park in Dallas, Texas, about the continuing relevance of *Animal Farm*. I was glad to hear one of them say, "I'd hate to lose it as required reading. It is such a great story, told with precious touches of humor." Another added, "It's [a] rare classic that students really enjoy." A thoughtful teacher told me, "The book is talking about any concentration of power. Last year [a] bright student suggested that 'the story warns us not to fight for our rights as students and then let class officers impose their ideas on the rest of us.'"

After a lecture, Bernard Crick, one of Orwell's biographers, was asked by a listener, "If Orwell were alive today, what would he be?" Crick's answer sidestepped the questioner's effort to pull Orwell politically to the right or to the left and put a tag on him. "If Orwell were alive today," Crick said, "he would be a very old man; he would probably be counting the marbles in his head and hoping they were all there." Indeed, if Orwell were alive and well and had all his marbles he would be fighting as he did all the days of his brief life, writing against oppression and corruption wherever it exists, glad to know that the young are still reading and learning from *Animal Farm*.

Animal Farm Is About a
Failure of Communication

Robert A. Lee

Robert A. Lee is an author and literary critic.

In the following article, Robert A. Lee asserts that Animal Farm, *although it details events in twentieth-century Russian history, is meant to be a treatment of all revolutions. Lee states that Orwell's theme is the importance of objective truth, and his concern is the danger that those in control will manipulate language to obscure the truth.*

[The narrative of *Animal Farm*] sets up equivalents with the history of political action in Russia from roughly 1917 to the Second World War. Major and Snowball are [Vladimir] Lenin and [Leon] Trotsky; Napoleon is [Joseph] Stalin; and the warring farms and farmers around Manor Farm naturally come to stand for Germany (Frederick) and the Allies (Pilkington). Certain events in the story are said to represent events of history: The timber deal, in which Frederick later reneges on the animals, is of course the short-lived Russo-German alliance of 1939; the card game at the end of the book is supposed to represent the Teheran Conference following the war. The correlations are more elaborate than this, and while there are some inconsistencies in the precise political allegory it is notable that one need pay little heed to this to understand the book in its full political significance. Instead of being just an allegory of twentieth-century Russian politics, *Animal Farm* is more meaningfully an anatomy of all political revolutions. As [critic] A.E. Dyson says, *Animal Farm* "is by no means about Russia alone. Orwell is concerned to

Robert A. Lee, "*Animal Farm*," in *Orwell's Fiction*, Notre Dame, IN: University of Notre Dame Press, 1969, pp. 105–127. Copyright © 1969 by University of Notre Dame Press. Reproduced by permission.

show how revolutionary ideals of justice, equality and fraternity always shatter in the event." I would submit that the implications of this little book are wider yet: It is not merely that revolutions are self-destructive—Orwell also is painting a grim picture of the human condition in the political twentieth century, a time which he has come to believe marks the end of the very concepts of human freedom. . . .

Failure to Live Up to Ideals

The book is . . . constructed on a circular basis. Major's speech builds to the rhetorical climax of "All animals are comrades," which apothegm is immediately punctuated by the dogs' pursuit of some rats that they see. A vote is taken and the rats become "comrades," followed by the animals banding together against their common enemy, man, under the aegis of the motto, "All animals are equal." The remainder of the book will be a series of dramatic repudiations of these mottoes, a return to the tyranny and irresponsibility of the beginning. The only change will be in the identity of the masters, and, ironically, even that will be only partially changed.

At the opening of the second chapter Major dies, the prophet who articulated the revolutionary ideals and in whose name they will be carried out—and perverted. Snowball and Napoleon, two pigs, assume the leadership of the rebellion, aided by their public-relations man, Squealer. And these three codify the ideals of Major into Animalism, "a complete system of thought." But Animalism, obviously analogous to communism, is significantly instituted without any plan. The rebellion occurs spontaneously: Once again Jones neglects to feed the animals, who break into the barn for food when "they could stand it no longer." Jones and his hired man come in and the animals, "with one accord, though nothing of the kind had been planned beforehand," attack the men and chase them off the farm. "And so almost before they knew what was happening, the Rebellion had been successfully carried through: Jones was expelled, and the Manor Farm was theirs." Orwell stresses the spontaneity of the Rebellion to make clear that the social revolution *per se* is not the object of his satire. He emphasizes that no matter how bad things become for the animals later—and they do become bad—the animals "were far better off than they had been in the days of Jones." Though this fact will itself have to be qualified, there is a justness in the statement. Not only does the revolution's spontaneity diminish the importance of Napoleon and Snowball's plotting— and thus provide a dramatic irony about their supposed accomplishments—but the motive, hunger, justifies the revolution more basically and irrefutably than the soundest of political theories. The revolution sprung, not from theory, but from real, natural need. No matter how corrupt the ideals of the revolution become, Orwell never questions the validity of the uprising: The target here is not social—and socialistic— revolution, contrary to the many who simply want to see the book as a satire of communism, but rather the target is the inability of humans to live within a community of ideals.

The inevitable corruption of the revolution is presaged immediately. The animals have driven out their former masters.

> For the first few minutes the animals could hardly believe in their good fortune. Their first act was to gallop in a body right round the boundaries of the farm, as though to make quite sure that no human being was hiding anywhere upon it; then they raced back to the farm buildings to wipe out the last traces of Jones's hated reign. The harness-room at the end of the stables was broken open; the bits, the nose-rings, the dog-chains, the cruel knives with which Mr. Jones had been used to castrate the pigs and lambs, were all flung down the well. The reins, the halters, the blinkers, the degrading nosebags, were thrown on to the rubbish fire which was burning in the yard. So were the whips. All the animals capered with joy when they saw the whips going up in flames.

The reaction is understandable; but the description of the inevitable and immediate violence that seems to follow all revolutions foreshadows that this revolution will suffer the common fate of its genre: reactionary cruelty, the search for the scapegoat, the perversion of the ideals of the revolution, and the counter-revolution. Thus, the good intentions of the animals are immediately endangered when it is learned that the pigs "had taught themselves to read and write from an old spelling book which had belonged to Mr. Jones's children." The pigs' reading ability is a valuable skill for the animals, one which is necessary to run a farm, even for animals. But it is also patently a human attribute, and one which already violates one of Major's cardinal tenets: "Remember also that in fighting against Man, we must not come to resemble him."

If seeds of destruction are immediately present, the positive aspects of the rebellion achieve their high peak with the codification of the "unalterable law by which all the animals on Animal Farm must live for ever after," the Seven Commandments.

1. Whatever goes upon two legs is an enemy.
2. Whatever goes upon four legs, or has wings, is a friend.
3. No animal shall wear clothes.
4. No animal shall sleep in a bed.
5. No animal shall drink alcohol.
6. No animal shall kill any other animal.
7. All animals are equal.

This "unalterable law" provides the major structural basis for the rest of the fable. From this point on the plot reveals a gradual alteration of these commandments, ending in the well-known contradiction that epitomizes the new nature of the farm at the end of the book. . . .

The Loss of Truth

It is not the threat of violence, even the radically inexplicable self-violence which the deracinated [uprooted] individual must, ironically, bring upon himself for his own secular salvation in a wholly political world, nor the war, nor the social injustice that man is suffering that is the cancer of our times, but the loss of "objective truth." Choices vanish in a society which has no bases for choice.

The most darkly pessimistic aspect of *Animal Farm* is that the animals are unable even to recognize their new oppression, much less combat it. The difference is that the pigs control language; Mr. Jones controlled only action—not thought. Orwell portrays at least three animals as being potentially able to stand up to the state (in an admittedly limited yet meaningful way), yet each is inadequate in a vital respect. Boxer has probably enough power and strength to overthrow Napoleon's regime. When Napoleon's vicious dogs attack him, Boxer simply "put out his great hoof, caught a dog in midair, and pinned him to the ground. The dog shrieked for mercy and the other two fled with their tails between their legs." But Boxer is stupid; he cannot comprehend the present, much less conceptualize the past. He ingenuously looks to Napoleon to see whether or not he should let the dog go; when the slaughter is over, he retreats to work, thinking the fault must lie within the animals. Thus, his fate is not as pathetic, as some critics read the scene in which he is taken away, kicking in the truck, as it is the inevitable fate of utter stupidity. The most complex thought that Boxer can express is "if Comrade Napoleon says it, it must be right," in the face of blatant, gross falsification. Boxer's basic goodness, social self-sacrifice, and impressive strength are simply inadequately used; the stupidity which wastes them suggests interesting qualifications about Orwell's reputed love of the common man, qualifications which become even stronger when considered in light of the descriptions of the proles in *1984*.

Clover is more intelligent and perceptive than is Boxer, but she has a corresponding lack of strength. Her "character" is primarily a function of her sex: Her instincts are maternal and pacifistic. She works hard, along with the other animals, but there is no picture of any special strength, as there is with Boxer. And even with a greater intelligence, her insights are partial. Things may indeed be better than they "had been in the days of Jones," but, in the context of the slaughter of the animals, "it was not for this that she and all the other animals had hoped and toiled." Both perceptions are right, but both are incomplete. In both cases, Clover senses that there is something further to be understood, but just as Boxer uncomprehendingly moves to toil, so does Clover wistfully retreat to song—only to have this articulation of the past's ideals suddenly changed, without her dissent. A paradigm appears: Boxer is marked by great strength and great stupidity; Clover has less physical power but has a corresponding increase in awareness; the equation is completed with Benjamin, who sees and knows most—perhaps all—but is physically ineffectual and socially irresponsible.

Benjamin, the donkey, "was the oldest animal on the farm, and the worst tempered. He seldom talked, but when he did, it was usually to make some cynical remark. . . ." As archetypal cynic, Benjamin remains aloof and distant, refusing to meddle in the farm's affairs, but seeing all. He expresses no opinion about the rebellion; he works on Animal Farm "in the same slow, obstinate way" that he did on Manor Farm; he only remarks enigmatically that "Donkeys live a long time." Beneath the surface cynicism, he is, almost predictably, blessed with a heart of gold: He is devoted to Boxer, and it is he who discovers the plot to deliver Boxer to the glue maker. But Benjamin is essentially selfish, representing a view of human nature that is apolitical, and thus he can hardly be the voice of Orwell within the book, as some readers hold. To Benjamin, the social and political situation is irrelevant: Human nature suffers and prospers in the same degree, no matter who is the master. He believes "that things never had been, nor ever could be much better or much worse—hunger, hardship, and disappointment being, so he said, the unalterable law of life." We know too much about Orwell's social beliefs from other contexts to assume that Benjamin speaks for Orwell here. Yet, it is only fair to note that Benjamin sees most, knows most, is obviously the most intelligent and perceptive of all the animals on the farm, including the pigs. To a certain extent, he represents intelligence without the effectuating and necessary strength; perhaps more profoundly, he demonstrates the Orwellian heinous sin of irresponsible intelligence. The posture of assuming that only the very worst is inevitable in life, that change for the better is a delusion, and that the only alternative is a retreat into a social self-pity is exactly the posture from which Orwell presumptively jerks Gordon Comstock in *Keep the Aspidistra Flying*.

Little Awareness of the Past

With the means of opposition to Napoleon's totalitarian rule so portrayed, there is little suspense in the outcome of the situation the novel describes. Years pass. Jones dies in an inebriates' [drunkards'] home; Boxer and Snowball are forgotten by nearly all, for a new generation of animals has grown up. The situation on the farm is unchanged for most of the animals: The farm is more prosperous now, but the fruits of prosperity never pass beyond Napoleon and his comrades. And the attempt to judge whether the present situation is better or worse than it had been under Jones is fruitless.

> Sometimes the older ones among them racked their dim memories and tried to determine whether in the early days of the Rebellion, when Jones's expulsion was still recent, things had been better or worse than now. They could not remember. There was nothing with which they could compare their present lives: they had nothing to go upon except Squealer's lists of figures, which invariably demonstrated that everything was getting better and better.

Again, the condition itself is not as depressing as the loss of the rational criteria which allow evaluation. The denial of memory enables control of the present, and hence of the future.

"And yet the animals never gave up hope." For they do retain one ineradicable achievement: equality. "If they went hungry, it was not from feeding tyrannical human beings; if they worked hard, at least they worked for themselves. No creature among them went on two legs. No creature called any other 'Master.' All animals were equal." The social and economic hopes of the revolution may have become lost in the actualities of history, but the primary political gain of the revolution remains valid for the animals. Orwell articulates this one, final achievement of the animals. But within a page Squealer and Napoleon appear, walking on their hind legs. Yet even this sight is not the final violation of hope. Clover and Benjamin walk around to the barn to read the seventh commandment:

ALL ANIMALS ARE EQUAL BUT SOME ANIMALS ARE MORE EQUAL THAN OTHERS

After this, "it did not seem strange" that the pigs take the humans' newspapers, that the pigs dress like humans, invite neighboring humans in to feast and drink, that the name of the farm is changed back to Manor Farm, and that, in the final image of the book, the pigs become indistinguishable from the humans. The book has come full circle, and things are back as they were. If this is so, Benjamin's judgment becomes valid: Things do remain the same, never much worse, never much better; "hunger, hardship, and disappointment" are indeed the "unalterable law of life."

Power inevitably corrupts the best of intentions, apparently no matter who possesses the power: At the end, all the representatives of the various ideologies are indistinguishable—they are all pigs, all pigs are humans. Communism is no better and no worse than capitalism or fascism; the ideals of socialism were long ago lost in Clover's uncomprehending gaze over the farm. Religion is merely a toy for the corrupters, neither offensive nor helpful to master or slave. But perhaps more distressing yet is the realization that everyone, the good and the bad, the deserving and the wicked, are not only contributors to the tyranny, are not only powerless before it, but are unable to understand it. Boxer thinks that whatever Napoleon says is right; Clover can only vaguely feel, and cannot communicate, that things are not exactly right; Benjamin thinks that it is in the nature of the world that things go wrong. The potential hope of the book is finally expressed only in terms of ignorance (Boxer), wistful inarticulateness (Clover), or the tired, cynical belief that things never change (Benjamin). The inhabitants of this world seem to deserve their fate.

Corrupted Language Obscures Truth

One must finally ask, however, with all this despair and bleakness, what are the actual bases for the tyranny of Annual Farm. Is the terrorism of the dogs the most crucial aspect? Is it this that rules the animals? Boxer's power is seen as superior to this violence and force. Is the basis of the final despair the pessimistic belief in the helplessness of the mass of the animals? Orwell elsewhere states again and again his faith in the common people. It seems to me that the basis of this society's evil is the inability of its inhabitants to ascertain truth and that this is demonstrated through the theme of the corruption of language. So long as the animals cannot remember the past, because it is continually altered, they have no control over the present and hence over the future. A society which cannot control its language is, says Orwell, doomed to be oppressed in terms which deny it the very most elemental aspects of humanity: To live in a world which allows the revised form of the seventh commandment of Animal Farm is not merely to renounce the belief in the possibility of human equality, but in the blatant perversion of language, the very concept of objective reality is lost.

The mode by which the recognition of reality is denied is the corruption of language. When a society no longer maintains its language as a common basis by which value, idea, and fact are to be exchanged, those who control the means of communication have the most awful of powers—they literally can create the truth they choose.

Traditional Values Can Win Out over Self-Serving Politics

Richard I. Smyer

Richard I. Smyer was a literary critic, author, and educator.

Orwell's satire in Animal Farm *has two targets, according to Richard I. Smyer. Orwell satirizes political extremists as dangerous and misguided. It is naïve to believe that a revolution can free a society from its history, Smyer claims. Orwell is also rejecting the belief that political action brings no progress. Despite the sinister ending of* Animal Farm, *Smyer contends that the animals have made some limited improvements on the farm that have bettered their condition. In addition to its caution about the nature of those in power to exercise that power corruptly, Smyer asserts,* Animal Farm *also celebrates traditional values and suggests that they can be an antidote to dictatorship.*

The satire in *Animal Farm* has two important aims—both based on the related norms of limitation and moderation. First, *Animal Farm* exposes and criticizes extremist political attitudes as dangerous. On the one hand, it satirizes the mentality of the utopian revolutionary—the belief that through the conscious effort of a ruling elite a society can be suddenly severed from its past and fashioned into a new, rational system—by showing that the Apollonian dream of technological progress and reason's rule inevitably evokes the Dionysiac[1] reaction of barbaric unreason. Implicit in Snowball's vision of high-technology modernization is the extirpation [wiping

1. Referring to Apollo, the Greek god of philosophy and the arts and Dionysus, the Greek god of wine, ecstasy, and the irrational.

Richard I. Smyer, "Trees into Books, Books into Trees," in *"Animal Farm": Pastoralism and Politics*, Boston, MA: Twayne Publishers, 1988, pp. 96–133.

out] of the animals' recent agricultural identity as domesticated creatures and—if Boxer's goal of improving his mind is any indication, their eventual transformation into Swiftian Houyhnhnms. Instead, Snowball's futuristic incantations conjure up a Stone Age Yahoo[2]—the power-hungry and pleasure-loving Napoleon.

The other extreme attitude being satirically rejected is the nihilistic disbelief in any kind of progress resulting from political activism. Although neither biological nor industrial reality has kept pace with theory—the "expected" population explosion on the farm and its envisioned electrification—life is in some respects better. Toward the end of the narrative it appears that the animal community has insured its physical survival—the most basic of needs—by a noticeable increase in its number, and limited improvements on the original farm, such as the erection of a windmill for the traditional purpose of milling corn for profit, has made the farm a going concern from which the still toiling animals can at least derive a sense of collective achievement.

Gentle, Sympathetic Satire

The other general aim of *Animal Farm* as satire is to offer itself as an example of temperate, responsible criticism—in no way a rancorous verbal assault. . . . Orwell's satire will be no iconoclastic wrecking job on a Stalinist Russia whose people had been suffering so cruelly from the war and whose soldiers, under Stalin's leadership, were locked in desperate combat with the German invader even as *Animal Farm* was being written. That Orwell's assault is primarily on an idea, the extremist fantasy of technological utopianism devoid of hard work, and less a living creature, the commander in chief, is demonstrated during the most dramatic moment of Farmer Frederick's attack on the farm—the juxtaposition of the dyna-

2. The Houyhnhnms, a race of intelligent, gentle horses, and the Yahoos, a brutish race, appear in Jonathan Swift's *Gulliver's Travels*.

mited (symbolically castrated) windmill and the figure of Napoleon alone standing unbowed. . . .

[The] moderateness of Orwell's satire is reinforced by a treatment of time that encourages the reader's sympathetic understanding of the whole revolutionary experiment from its spontaneous and joyous beginnings to its ambiguous condition on the final page. . . . The fact that of all Orwell's separately published narratives, *Animal Farm*, the shortest in length, contains the longest time span between the first event of the narrated present and the last—a period of time greater than the four calendar years referred to by the narrator—allows the presentation of factors that to some extent implicitly explain and thus mitigate the follies and abuses of the revolution. Without a past to account for his present behavior, Don Quixote's deeds would be mere zaniness; with a past, the years spent poring over chivalric romances, his follies become humanly understandable, even noble. In *Animal Farm* the past that jolts the creatures from the timeless present of the animal condition into the manic state of historical consciousness is a quick, magically transformative moment—the past that Old Major springs on the other beasts during his nocturnal talk. And as mentioned in chapter 2 regarding Boxer's behavior, the fact that this introjected consciousness involves the vivid awareness of suffering and bloodshed—the animals being a collective sacrifice on the altar of profit—invests the narrative with an element of pathos that deepens satiric red into a tragic purple. This is not to say that a satiric code is not operant: Napoleon is the conniving, knavish master of Juvenalian [as in the Roman poet Juvenal's works] satire; Squealer is still the satiric servant all too willing to carry out his master's evil schemes, as is shown by his glibly pseudoscientific justification for the brain-working pigs' hogging of the milk and apple rations; and the subject beasts remain gulls. Nevertheless, the nagging thought that Jones could return—not only Jones the individual at the terrifying center or the animals' recently acquired historical consciousness but also countless Jones types armed with noose and knife—encourages the writer and the reader alike to balance satiric mockery with sympathy. . . .

An Allegorical Warning

As an allegorical warning against the wartime Soviet ally, *Animal Farm* is in the spirit of John Gay's "The Gardener and the Hog" (1727), a fable in which a gardener's pet hog, drunk from ale (like Orwell's Napoleon), tramples down the garden and then slashes the too trusting youth's leg—the moral being that he "who cherishes a brutal mate / Shall mourn the folly soon or late." A good example of what Orwell was up against was a directive from the British Ministry of Information to Orwell and other BBC news broadcasters during the war. Headed "Arguments to counter the ideological fear of 'Bolshevism,'" the directive's gist is that the BBC should play up the purported virtues of the Soviet Union—its scientific and cultural advances, its encouragement of individual initiative and ownership of private property, and its tolerance toward religion and rejection of international revolutionary activity, as well as the unlikelihood of its gaining control of Europe—while branding any negative views as Nazi propaganda. Given Orwell's interest in keeping British socialism free of authoritarian foreign influences, and the fact that by 1945 a general election would have to take place in England (an election that might put in power the only major party receptive to socialist programs, Labor), it is understandable that "The Freedom of the Press"—an essay written in 1944 or 1945 as an introduction to *Animal Farm* but in fact not published with it—would define the writer's liberty as the "right to tell people what they do not want to hear." Orwell's message to Labor was to accept the Fabian [Trojan] horse within the gates but to make sure it concealed no Stalinist shock troops.

Not surprisingly, two important themes conveyed through the allegory are incognizance, a lack of information or awareness, and the perfidy of associates. Not only are the important truths not known, often both beast and man attempt to block them from consciousness. Stupefied with alcohol, Farmer Jones can sink into the depths of sleep unmindful of his mate's snoring and the implicit commentary the sound is making on the marriage, and Napoleon's drunken condition makes it easier for him to don Jones's hat without having to face the full implications of this action in relation to his animal identity. The roar of the shotgun that temporarily restores Jones's farmyard world to its normal identity is a parallel to the "tremendous bleeting" of the sheep that quashes rational debate regarding Snowball's expulsion. The conscious and willing assumption of a political, revolutionary identity is either cause or effect of the mark of Cain branded into the leaders' behavior: one look at Snowball's engineering plans is enough to turn Napoleon's recent comrade-in-arms into a rival that must be destroyed; Napoleon has no qualms about selling timber to Frederick, whom the animals loathe above all other human beings for his sadism—and who shamelessly uses the deal to defraud Napoleon; reasonably expecting to be rewarded for his labors with a leisurely retirement, old Boxer is sold to the horse-slaughterer; and that betrayal is becoming the norm is indicated by the cheating at cards during the pigs' and human beings' unity banquet.

An allegorical view of reality—the thing said or displayed really meaning something else—suited the Marxist-oriented social criticism of the 1930s, which was indefatigable in pointing out the economically self-serving motives underlying the surface features of modern bourgeois society. . . .

A Balanced Society

Animal Farm embodies a double vision of society—society as a stage or arena for the display of an elite group's or a dominant individual's increasingly extreme self-regarding behavior and, on the other hand, as a commonplace setting for the muted celebration of communal values. In *Animal Farm* some of the world, but not all, is a stage, and the ascendancy of the porcine leaders owes as much to their flair for the dramatic, their seemingly innate theatricality, as to their braininess. The pigs are drawn to the stage and its tricks. Speaking from a raised platform, Old Major holds the attention of his late-night audience by first mentioning the "strange dream" that the animals have assembled to hear about and then delaying an account of it until after having lectured his sleepy listeners into a state of suggestibility. "Skipping from side to side and whisking his tail" while explaining away porcine selfishness as selfless statesmanship, Squealer is perfecting a propagandistic song-and-dance act. It is fair to assume that in Snowball's mind the most delightful feature of the leisure society he en-visions is the free time the other animals will have to give ear to his "brilliant speeches". Napoleon is the most Machiavellian pig's name, and histrionics—not just history—is his game: an Eisenstein's Ivan the Terrible [a notorious Russian czar] in his periods of brooding bursting into fits of rage (the film biogra-phy [of Ivan by Sergei Eisenstein] having appeared in 1942), the bemedalled and strutting Napoleon is also the pompous ruler of [Charlie] Chaplin's *The Great Dictator* (1940). And the animals seem destined for certain roles and fates by the names given them by Farmer Jones or some other human be-ing. Named Boxer, what else could an Edwardian draft horse expect out of life but some form of martyrdom? Some ob-scure martial passion must have been stirred into life by the change of name from "the Willingdon Beauty" to "Old Ma-jor"; the curious career of Snowball—the cyclic expansion and contraction of his real or imaginary power—is there freeze dried in his name; and the English farmer who would name one vigorous young boar Napoleon without raising another one named the Duke of Wellington [who defeated Napoleon Bonaparte] was asking for trouble.

On a flyleaf of Orwell's copy of [Peter Drucker's] *The Future of Industrial Man* is a page reference to a passage in Drucker's book defining the range of meaningful sociopolitical freedom, and after the page reference is the following comment (in what appears to be Orwell's hand): "Man is not only his brother's keeper, he is his brother's brother." Rather than a sentimental tautology, this statement, with its allusion to the stormy relationships of biblical brothers, calls attention to what may be the central motif of *Animal Farm* as political commentary—the inevitable transformation of association into enmity. Entry into political history is a journeying into a [Thomas] Hobbesian state of nature ruled by rivalry, distrust, and betrayal. But if this were all there were to *Animal Farm*, it would be for writer and for reader a "header into the cesspool" of political pornography. Instead, however, it is a bipolar narrative, the literary counterpart of a balanced society, in which political allegory, although important, is held in check by other modes of experience.

The Animal as Literary Beast of Burden

A basic satiric assumption about animals is that they are suitable devices for presenting man as ridiculous or brutal, and Orwell's narratives of the early thirties are studded with examples of animal imagery used by Orwell and his characters for purposes of satiric reduction. However, toward the end of the decade, when the harsh spotlight of Orwell's reductive satire was tending to shade off into the deeper tones of a philosophical pessimism mixed with compassion, his animal imagery came to be used as a means of evoking for his flawed and vulnerable human characters some of the positive feelings spontaneously and unconditionally awakened in us by animals. Any conclusions regarding the use of animal imagery in *Animal Farm* for debunking and reductive purposes should take into account not only Orwell's deepening interest in animals in their own right in the later thirties (feelings owing in part to his farming activities at Wallington) but also the expanded meanings associated with animal imagery. In the long essay "The Lion and the Unicorn: Socialism and the English Genius," written in 1941, one of the darkest periods of British history, Orwell's faith in the nation's ability to survive is metaphorically linked to an essential animality: "The Stock Exchange will be pulled down, the horse plough will give way to the tractor . . . the Eton and Harrow match will be forgotten, but England will still be England, an everlasting animal stretching into the future and the past, and, like all living things, having the power to change out of recognition and yet remain the same." The unspoken message of *Animal Farm* is that England will weather the storms of the postwar world only if the English people do not cease believing in England and Englishness as a living, enduring creature. In terms of allegorical dualism of Orwell's beast fable, the pigs are positioned at the land's end of the familiar reality being changed "out of recognition," while the humbler animals, never giving up hope, collectively embody a national determination to "remain the same." If the extreme political humanization of the pigs fixes the reader's attention on the transformative power of futuristic, city-generated ideologies, the very limited and apparently temporary political humanization of the other farm creatures—a humanness usually balanced by reminders of animality (such as the tendency to experience reality as a permanent present, the predominance of biological needs, freedom as the ability to act in accordance with species-specific behavioral patterns)—awakens a reader's romantic nostalgia for a happier rural past. . . .

Pastoral and Political Allegory

Two impulses at work in *Animal Farm* are the politically allegorical, the exposure of the totalitarian nature of a specifically Stalinist and generally Bonapartist socialism and the pastoral—the latter term including a number of literary conventions and themes resonant enough to expand the reader's focus from the narrowly political and topical to the broadly archetypal. It should be noted that political allegorization is a development that takes place somewhere during the course of the narrative as a whole and never entirely absorbs the story. The opening scene of the tipsy Jones could just as well introduce a comically realistic novel of farm life, and even the assembly of animals of different species able to understand another animal's utterances accords with the conventions of the animal story. Only when Old Major veers away from the simple description of his dream, an experience basic enough to be immediately understood by fowl and mammal alike, to a polemical rhetoric dealing with the alienation of animals from human beings that events invite an allegorical interpretation. And even then the futuristic vision that grips the animals' imagination is of an essentially nonallegorical condition—of a world that, being without human beings, could not be allegorical in the accepted sense of the term. Conditioned by Old Major's political rhetoric, readers (including this writer) sometimes mistakenly regard the first violent confrontation of man and animal—the hunger-driven animals' breaking into the feed shed and their instinctively self-protective reaction to the men's attack—as a political and therefore politically allegorical event. However, it is not until around the time of the second violent encounter that the behavior of the animals exhibits qualities that are humanly political—the creation of a command structure, goal-directed planning, the development of both an organizational consciousness and an inspiriting ethos precisely formulated in terms of a guiding ideology. . . .

Animal Farm as Parable

In *Animal Farm* cyclic imagery is associated with the moral dangers of an obsessive revolutionary activism. The Napoleon racing drunkenly around the farmyard is a creature imprisoned in his own egocentric craving for power. That an atmosphere of senseless violence may be spreading to the humbler animals' imaginations—perhaps even to their actual behavior—is suggested by the sheep's confession of having chased a sickly old ram around a bonfire until he died. If the windmill is tightly bound up with Snowball's tempting vision of an electrified and effortless paradise, the turning blades signify history's inconstancy, with the bend sinister of primitive impulse turning the revolutionary propagandist's progressive futuristic myth of unidirectional movement into at best a flattened upward spiral.

The general movement of *Animal Farm* is toward a division of the animal community into those creatures mired in the pitch of worldliness—the pigs (as well as their human counterparts) gripped by a craving at all costs to gain the upper hand by displaying a winning one—and those beasts who maintain a balance between a proud attachment to their unique social experiment and a basically passive, quietist acceptance of their workaday existence as toilers working their collective half acre. The widening gap in the narrative between the politically allegorized pigs and the producing beasts drawing back into their ancient identities of domesticated animality becomes a parabolic [parable-like] field. From the honeyed and then rancorous utterances of the mutually suspicious groups of schemers inside the farmhouse and the puzzled silence of the unnoticed spectators in the farmyard arises the implicit lesson that to save its collective soul England (and by extension the democratic West) must preserve the pastoral qualities of acceptance and endurance as a check on the restless craving of modern revolutionary man for ever more extreme—and therefore ultimately self-subverting—political goals.

Contemporary
Perspectives on Politics

Debates on the Size of Government Should Be Conducted Rationally

Cathy Young

Cathy Young writes a weekly column for the Web site RealClear-Politics and is also a contributing editor for the libertarian Reason magazine.

In the following viewpoint, Cathy Young claims that far-right conservatives who brand President Barack Obama as a Communist are simply wrong. More moderate conservatives depict Obama's policies as similar to those of "European-style" socialism—specifically a European type of welfare state—and caution against the dangers of introducing such a system into the United States. While Young describes Obama as a proponent of an activist government, she points out that the U.S. government became bigger under George W. Bush's Republican administration. Young asserts that there is a reasonable debate to be had about the role of government and urges each side in the political conversation to refrain from harmful exaggeration about the other.

A specter is stalking America—the specter of socialism.

The once-neglected S-word made a big comeback during the presidential campaign of 2008, and has now become a staple of American political discourse. While the right denounces [Barack] Obama as a socialist, the cover of *Newsweek* magazine proclaims, "We are all socialists now." Is he? Are we? Depends on how you define "socialism," of course.

Obama a Communist?

For Obama's more strident detractors, the label is practically synonymous with "communist." Back in October [2008], *Wash-*

Cathy Young, "Are We All Socialists Now?" *RealClearPolitics*, March 4, 2009. Reproduced by permission.

ington Times columnist Jeffery T. Kuhner predicted that Obama's victory would usher in "the U.S.S.A."—the United Socialist States of America. This catchy phrase is now showing up on bumper stickers, along with the self-explanatory moniker, "Comrade Obama."

This kind of rhetoric is not just the province of marginal firebrands. *The New York Times* reports that, speaking at the Conservative Political Action Conference in Washington [the weekend of February 28, 2009], Mike Huckabee, former Governor of Arkansas and presidential contender, fulminated about the creation of "socialist republics" in America and asserted that "[Vladimir] Lenin and [Joseph] Stalin would love this stuff."

To those who remember the murderous horror that was the USSR [Union of Soviet Socialist Republics, or the Soviet Union], this flippant use of Communist and Soviet analogies should be deeply offensive, indeed obscene—the right-wing equivalent of the leftist habit of flinging Nazi metaphors at conservatives. Lenin, Stalin and Obama are as much of a trio as [Adolf] Hitler, [Benito] Mussolini and [George W.] Bush. Lenin and Stalin did not want to tax the rich a little more; they wanted to confiscate all their property and either kill them or send them to concentration camps (and to eliminate all political opposition and independent opinion).

Less wild-eyed critics acknowledge that the socialism they invoke is the "European-style" variety—in other words, not the system of our totalitarian Cold War enemy but that of our democratic allies. This is not to say that European-style socialism is something we should embrace, only that it's not a particularly terrifying bogeyman.

Is Obama a champion of European-style socialism—or, more precisely, a European-style welfare state? It is safe to say that, his protestations notwithstanding, he does not dislike bigger government. Conservative Obama supporters such as *New York Times* columnist David Brooks now complain that

Obama is not the moderate they took him to be and that his view of government is far more aggressive than they expected. (What made them expect Obama to be anything but a proponent of activist government is unclear.)

Government Grew Under Bush

The problem is that Republicans are not exactly on solid ground in denouncing Obama's proposed government expansion—not after colluding in the Bush Administration's spending spree. A headline in *The Weekly Standard* warns of "The Return of Big Government"; but big government never left, and certainly not under Bush. Obama may be seeking to reverse Ronald Reagan's legacy; but, as conservative economist Bruce Bartlett argued persuasively in his 2006 book, *Impostor*, that legacy was already betrayed by Bush. Many people will tell you we officially became "the U.S.S.A." with the bank bailout in October 2008.

The United States may have a substantially smaller welfare state than European nations, but we have not had anything resembling "pure capitalism" for a very long time. Neither Reagan nor the Republican Congress were able to substantially reverse government growth. Social Security and Medicare are "socialism," and whatever their (substantial) economic flaws, they have proved politically untouchable; a major expansion of Medicare—prescription drug coverage for seniors—was enacted on Bush's watch. Even outside Medicare the American health care system is no "free market" but an often unwieldy mix of market and regulation. Obama's proposed education initiatives expand, but hardly revolutionize, the federal role.

Conservative activist Matt Kibbe told the *New York Times* that "Americans are just genetically opposed to socialism." But if we're talking about the kind of "socialism" we are likely to get, this statement is (like it or not) as much in the realm of wishful thinking as the "Obamacons'" faith in Obama's commitment to limited government.

No sane person today would argue the merits of communism or Soviet-style socialism vs. democratic capitalism. But the size and role of government in democratic capitalist societies is very much a subject of legitimate debate. Most people favor some balance between security and flexibility, more equality and more individual opportunity. We proponents of small government should be able to argue for flexibility and opportunity without painting the other side as evil—and to criticize the Democrats' proposals without resorting to a Red Scare.

Of course, demonization cuts both ways. Fairly modest Republican attempts to curb the welfare state have been habitually painted by Democrats as plans to starve orphans and throw grandmas out on the street. Now, we have Republicans equating federal student aid with the gulag [Soviet prison camp]. Reasoned debate in politics? More wishful thinking.

The United States Is Becoming Fascist Rather than Socialist

Jonah Goldberg

Jonah Goldberg is a member of USA Today's *board of contributors and the author of* Liberal Fascism: The Secret History of the American Left, from Mussolini to the Politics of Change.

In the following viewpoint, Jonah Goldberg argues that, despite compelling evidence that the U.S. government is taking an ever-larger role in controlling more and more aspects of the lives of its citizens, liberals claim conservatives are being paranoid when they warn of an age of socialism. According to Goldberg, political commentators from both sides admit that Barack Obama's administration is steering the country toward socialism or social democracy. Goldberg points out that many liberal politicians and commentators even seem to favor such policies yet persist in denying that the Democratic Party is becoming increasingly socialist. In reality, he concludes, the joint policy making of government and corporations resembles not socialism but fascism.

Tell liberals that the U.S. is headed toward—well, you know—and they laugh it off as political paranoia. So how to explain the sometimes subtle, yet often bold, advocacy of a socialist system?

The government effectively owns General Motors and controls Chrysler, and the president is deciding what kind of cars they can make. Uncle Sam owns majority stakes in American International Group [AIG], Fannie Mae, Freddie Mac and controls large chunks of the banking industry. Also, President [Barack] Obama wants government to take over the business of student loans. And he's pushing for nationalized health care. Meanwhile, his Environmental Protection Agency has ruled that it reserves the right to regulate any economic activity that has a "carbon footprint." Just last week [in May 2009], House Speaker Nancy Pelosi said climate change requires that "every aspect of our lives must be subjected to an inventory." Rep. Barney Frank, chair of the Financial Services Committee, has his eye on regulating executive pay.

Of course, nationalization of industry is only one kind of socialism; another approach is to simply redistribute the nation's income as economic planners see fit. But wait, Obama believes in that, too. That's why he said during the campaign that he wants to "spread the wealth"—and that's why he did exactly that when he got elected. (He spread the debt, too.)

And yet, for conservatives to suggest in any way, shape or form that there's something "socialistic" about any of this is the cause of knee-slapping hilarity for liberal pundits and bloggers everywhere.

For instance, [in May 2009] the Republican National Committee [RNC] considered a resolution calling on the Democratic Party to rename itself the "Democrat Socialist Party." The resolution was killed by RNC Chairman Michael Steele in favor of the supposedly milder condemnation of the Democrats' "march toward socialism."

The Hope for Socialism

The whole spectacle was just too funny for liberal observers. Robert Schlesinger, *U.S. News & World Report's* opinion editor, was a typical giggler. He chortled, "What's really both funny and scary about all of this is how seriously the fringe-nuts in the GOP [Grand Old Party: Republicans] take it." Putting aside the funny and scary notion that it's "funny and scary" for political professionals to take weighty political issues seriously, there are some fundamental problems with all of this disdain. For starters, why do liberals routinely suggest, even hope, that Obama and the Democrats are leading us into an age of socialism, or social democracy or democratic socialism? (One source of confusion is that these terms are routinely used interchangeably.)

For instance, in (another) fawning interview with President Obama, *Newsweek* editor Jon Meacham mocks Obama's critics for considering Obama to be a "crypto-socialist." This, of course, would be the same Jon Meacham who [in] February [2009] co-authored a cover story with *Newsweek*'s editor at large (and grandson of the six-time presidential candidate for the American Socialist Party) Evan Thomas titled—wait for it—"We Are All Socialists Now," in which they argued that the growth of government was making us like a "European," i.e. socialist, country.

Washington Post columnists Jim Hoagland (a centrist), E.J. Dionne (a liberal) and Harold Meyerson (very, very liberal) have all suggested that Obama intentionally or otherwise is putting us on the path to "social democracy." Left-wing blogger and Democratic activist Matthew Yglesias [in fall 2008] hoped that the financial crisis offered a "real opportunity" for "massive socialism." Polling done by Rasmussen—and touted by Meyerson—shows that while Republicans favor "capitalism" over "socialism" by 11 to 1, Democrats favor capitalism by a mere 39% to 30%. So, again: Is it really crazy to think that there is a constituency for some flavor of socialism in the Democratic Party?

When the question is aimed at them like an accusation, liberals roll their eyes at such "paranoia." They say Obama is merely reviving "New Deal economics" to "save" or "reform" capitalism. But liberals themselves have long seen this approach as the best way to incrementally bring about a European-style, social democratic welfare state. As Arthur Schlesinger Jr. (Robert's father) wrote in 1947, "There seems no inherent obstacle to the gradual advance of socialism in the United States through a series of New Deals."

Where to Draw the Line

Part of the problem here is definitional. No mainstream liberal actually wants government to completely seize the means of production, and no mainstream conservative believes that there's no room for any government regulation or social insurance. Both sides believe in a "mixed economy" but disagree profoundly about where to draw the line. One definition of social democracy is the peaceful, democratic transition to socialism. A second is simply a large European welfare state where the state owns some, and guides the rest, of the economy. Many liberals yearn for the latter and say so often—but fume when conservatives take them at their word.

Personally, I think socialism is the wrong word for all of this. "Corporatism"—the economic doctrine of fascism—fits better. Under corporatism, all the big players in the economy—big business, unions, interest groups—sit around the table with government at the head, hashing out what they think is best for everyone to the detriment of consumers, markets and entrepreneurs. But, take it from me, liberals are far more open to the argument that they're "crypto-socialists."

Liberalism, Not Socialism, Is on the Rise

Alan Wolfe

Alan Wolfe is a political scientist and sociologist who teaches at Boston College. He is director of the Boisi Center for Religion and American Public Life and a member of the Advisory Board of the Future of American Democracy Foundation. Wolfe is also the author of some twenty books and a contributing editor to the New Republic, Commonwealth, In Character, *and the* Wilson Quarterly.

In the following viewpoint, Alan Wolfe contends that those who are claiming socialism is on the rise are wrong. What is on the rise is liberalism, which is not the same as socialism. The major difference between the two is in their approach to individual liberty, Wolfe explains. The goal of liberalism is to offer personal autonomy to all, typically through government intervention. Socialists want as much equality as possible, even at the expense of individual liberty. The Obama administration is a liberal administration and is no more socialist than the administration of George W. Bush, Wolfe argues.

The word "liberal" was first used in its modern political sense in 1812, when Spaniards wrote a new constitution liberating themselves from monarchical rule. As it happens, the word "socialism" originated in roughly the same period; it came into existence to describe the utopian ideas of the British reformer Robert Owen. Such timing suggests two possibilities: Either the fates of liberalism and socialism are so inter-

Alan Wolfe, "Obama vs. Marx," *The New Republic*, vol. 240, no. 5, April 1, 2009, pp. 21–23. Copyright © 2009 by The New Republic, Inc. Reproduced by permission of *The New Republic*.

linked that one is all but synonymous with the other—or the two are actually competitors developed to meet similar conditions, in which case victory for one marks the defeat of the other.

Conditions No Longer Exist

These days, one could be forgiven for believing that the former conclusion is correct. It was not so long ago that conservatives were equating liberalism with fascism; today, they have executed a 180-degree swing in order to argue that liberalism is actually synonymous with socialism. "Americans," proclaimed Republican Senator Jim DeMint at the recent meeting of the Conservative Political Action Conference, "have gotten a glimpse of the big-government plans of [Barack] Obama and the Democrats and are ready to stand up, speak out, and, yes, even to take to the streets to stop America's slide into socialism." But it isn't just the right that has worked itself into a frenzy; on the question of whether we are approaching a new age of socialism, there seems to be remarkable political consensus. In recent weeks, the covers of *National Review* ("Our Socialist Future"), *The Nation* ("Reinventing Capitalism, Reimaging Socialism"), and *Newsweek* ("We Are All Socialists Now") have—respectively—lamented, heralded, and observed the coming rise of socialism.

But all these commentators—right, left, and middle—may want to take a deep breath. We aren't headed for an era of socialism at all, since socialism is not a natural outgrowth of liberalism. Liberalism is a political philosophy that seeks to extend personal autonomy to as many people as possible, if necessary through positive government action; socialism, by contrast, seeks as much equality as possible, even if doing so curtails individual liberty. These are differences of kind, not degree—differences that have historically placed the two philosophies in direct competition. Today, socialism is on the decline, in large part because liberalism has lately been on the rise. And, if Barack Obama's version of liberalism succeeds, socialism will be even less popular than it already is.

Socialism was born in political conditions that no longer exist. In its most radical form, the one associated with [Karl] Marx and [Friedrich] Engels, it had far more in common with European romanticism than with the moderate reformism of a John Stuart Mill or a Thomas Hill Green, two of Great Britain's most important liberal thinkers. Socialism seemed possible when anything seemed possible. It was an ideology of progress when progress was an unquestioned good. Even its less revolutionary adherents, those more likely to call themselves social democrats rather than socialists, believed in economic planning and social transformation in ways that seem embarrassing now. Once it appeared possible for government to control the major means of production. Now it seems impossible to build a high-speed rail between Boston and Washington.

The story of socialism's decline is essentially a European story. Socialism has never had much appeal in the United States, but that was not always the case on the other side of the Atlantic. The temptation toward socialism was not just on display in Eastern Europe; in the western half of the continent, too, left-wing governments and parties quite openly embraced socialist programs for much of the twentieth century. Those days, however, are largely over. In Britain, the Labour Party no longer pays much homage to its socialist roots. [Former prime minister] Tony Blair revived the party only after leading a campaign to alter its notorious Clause IV, which had explicitly endorsed the "common ownership of the means of production." The revised version proclaimed Labour a "democratic socialist" party, but the wording was so vague, and Blair so consistently ignored it, that its purposes were symbolic only. On this crucial point, [Blair's successor] Gordon Brown has not backtracked in the least.

Elsewhere in Europe, the same movement against socialism dominates the political landscape. Socialism in the form of social democracy was long the governing ideology of Scandinavia, but Swedes never much liked the idea of nationalizing industries, and the Danes have for some time been governed by conservatives—called, in European parlance, liberals. [Germany's chancellor] Angela Merkel is anything but a socialist; the same is true for [France's president] Nicolas Sarkozy. "Americanization" was once a dirty word in France. Now it fairly well describes Sarkozy's domestic program. There is talk of reforming the country's Napoleonic legal system with something more resembling our insistence upon rights. Public bureaucracies, including France's complex system of higher education, are to be reformed along more "modern"— read American—lines. Spain, meanwhile, does have a socialist government; but its leftism is a reaction to the extreme conservatism that governed the country for much of the twentieth century. For their part, the Eastern European countries now outdo each other in their love for the free market.

It is true that European societies are committed to an active role for government and that a number of their public policies, such as national health insurance, owe something to the socialist tradition. But the roots of the European welfare state are much more complex than is commonly acknowledged. European ideas about government have Christian as well as socialist origins. Two great papal encyclicals—*Rerum Novarum* (1891) and *Quadragesimo Anno* (1931)—spurred Catholic countries to adopt the idea that government should protect the rights of workers and that society has an obligation to help all. One of Great Britain's most eloquent defenders of equality, the Fabian socialist R.H. Tawney, was a devout Protestant. After World War II, Christian parties siphoned off votes that might have gone to more radical politicians by emphasizing traditions of solidarity and community. If Obama is really leading us down the road to Europeanization, an equally accurate *Newsweek* headline might be, "We Are All Christian Democrats Now."

And the origins of big government in Europe run deeper than either Marx[ist] or Christian politics. It is not exactly socialism that has stifled so much of French economic life with cumbersome regulations but a blunderbuss government that dates back to the *ancien régime* [the monarchy]. Socialist politicians in France did not invent the idea of big government. They instead relied on traditions of étatism that had long preceded them. Given all this, it's no wonder that liberalism is experiencing a comeback in Europe. The revival of liberal sentiment is as much a reaction against both Christianity and feudalism as anything else.

Obama Is Fixing Capitalism

As for Obama, it is absurd to view his program as a step toward socialism. First of all, while he is planning to raise taxes, they will still be lower than what is common in other Western countries. And, according to Brian Reidl of the Heritage Foundation, Obama's budget would increase government spending from 20 percent of GDP [gross domestic product] to 22 percent. Is it really possible that a society is capitalist when government spending represents 20 percent of GDP—but socialist at 22 percent?

Next, consider Obama's stances on the defining issues of our time. At most, his administration might nationalize banks temporarily; a socialist would nationalize them for good. He proposes to fix free trade, not abolish it. He does not favor a single-payer health care system, and any proposal he eventually puts forward is going to involve competition in some form. (It is worth noting that arguably the biggest beneficiaries of health care reform will be businesses, many of which struggle to pay their employees' health care costs.) To address

Barack Obama, elected U.S. senator from Illinois in 2004, became U.S. president in 2009. Some have labeled Obama's policies as socialist. AP Images.

global warming, Obama favors cap and trade, a market-oriented solution to our gravest environmental problem. That's right: This alleged socialist has so much faith in capitalism, he is willing to put the future of our planet more or less in the hands of a market.

What these ideas have in common is, first, an attachment to economic freedom that no self-respecting socialist would countenance. In fact, most of Obama's measures are designed to save, not destroy, the instruments of capitalism—businesses and the markets in which they compete. Should Obama get everything he wants, liberals will have once again—as has happened so often in the United States—gone a long way toward rescuing capitalism from its worst excesses.

Moreover, it has for some time now been established that the moderate use of government to improve the lives of large numbers of citizens, while producing minor advances in equality, is primarily about giving citizens more liberty. People who, with the help of government, need not postpone medical care or can avoid going into lifetime debt to pay for it are freer people. Progressive taxation, especially the way Obama talks about it, is not about confiscating the wealth of the rich but about giving those at the bottom of the ladder more opportunity. Modest enhancements of what has been called "positive liberty" do not come anywhere close to socialism; they instead make liberalism's benefits more widespread.

Conservatives seem to think that any increase in the size of government means a step toward socialism. But, if this is the case, then George W. Bush ought to come out of the closet as a socialist. It is not just that Bush spent uncountable sums on his Iraqi adventure. Nor is it that he put [late economics guru John Maynard] Keynes to shame by spending money he did not have. Bush, at least at the start of his presidency, wanted to be known for his compassion and sponsored reforms of both Medicare and education that, had a Democrat proposed them, would have been widely denounced by conservatives as socialism run rampant. Socialism, in the Republican imagination, is only something Democrats do, never something they themselves do.

In the United States, liberalism is the alternative to which we turn when conservatism fails, just as in Europe it is what people look to when socialism sputters, Christianity no longer appeals, and the old feudal statism appears moribund. Liberalism has always been more comfortable finding its place between the extremes than mimicking either one of them. Americans tend to be most familiar with the ways in which liberalism distinguishes itself from conservatism. But liberalism has gone to great lengths to distinguish itself from the left as well—from the gulag, the Soviet occupation of Eastern European countries against the will of their people, and all the various forms of socialism from Baathism [in Iraq] to Castroism [in Cuba] associated with Third World tyrants. These distinctions have reaffirmed the liberal dedication to human rights—and this at a time when conservatives like Bush and [former vice president Dick] Cheney were prepared to dispense with them. Conservatives may denounce Obama for his socialism, but it is he, and not they, who is returning the United States to such liberal commitments as the separation of powers, habeas corpus, and transparency in government.

If Barack Obama is a socialist, he sure is good at fooling people. Americans seem to like his quiet demeanor, his sense of caution, his efforts at inclusion. With its emphasis on intellectual modesty and pragmatism, liberalism is a temperament as well as a set of ideas; and Obama's disposition is quintessentially liberal.

We cannot at this point know what his legacy will be. But we do know what it will not be. Eight years of Obama, and the United States has its best chance in decades to return to the liberalism that has long defined its heritage. There would be no greater blow to socialism—in America, in Europe, or anywhere else—than for this venture to succeed.

Socialism Is Dying Out in Europe

Steven Erlanger

Steven Erlanger is the Paris bureau chief of the New York Times.

In the following viewpoint, Steven Erlanger asserts that socialism in Europe is on the wane, as evidenced by the defeat of left-leaning candidates in Germany, France, and Italy and by the vulnerable position of left-leaning governments in Spain and England. Conservatives are coming to power because they have adopted some of the more popular programs of the left—such as welfare, health care, and environmental protection—and are combining these with promises of a more efficient government with lower taxes. Socialists need to make significant changes to their programs if they are to remain a relevant party in Europe, Erlanger suggests.

Paris—A specter is haunting Europe—the specter of Socialism's slow collapse.

Even in the midst of one of the greatest challenges to capitalism in 75 years, involving a breakdown of the financial system due to "irrational exuberance," greed and the weakness of regulatory systems, European Socialist parties and their left-wing cousins have not found a compelling response, let alone taken advantage of the right's failures.

German voters clobbered the Social Democratic Party on Sunday, giving it only 23 percent of the vote, its worst performance since World War II.

Voters also punished left-leaning candidates in the summer's European Parliament elections and trounced French

Steven Erlanger, "Europe's Socialists Suffering Even in Downturn," *The New York Times*, September 29, 2009, p. A1. Copyright © 2009 by The New York Times Company. Reproduced by permission.

Socialists in 2007. Where the left holds power, as in Spain and Britain, it is under attack. Where it is out, as in France, Italy and now Germany, it is divided and listless.

Some American conservatives demonize President Obama's fiscal stimulus and health care overhaul as a dangerous turn toward European-style Socialism—but it is Europe's right, not left, that is setting its political agenda.

Europe's center-right parties have embraced many ideas of the left: generous welfare benefits, nationalized health care, sharp restrictions on carbon emissions, the ceding of some sovereignty to the European Union. But they have won votes by promising to deliver more efficiently than the left, while working to lower taxes, improve financial regulation, and grapple with aging populations.

Europe's conservatives, says Michel Winock, a historian at the Paris Institut d'Études Politiques, "have adapted themselves to modernity." When Nicolas Sarkozy of France and Germany's Angela Merkel condemn the excesses of the "Anglo-Saxon model" of capitalism while praising the protective power of the state, they are using Socialist ideas that have become mainstream, he said.

It is not that the left is irrelevant—it often represents the only viable opposition to established governments, and so benefits, as in the United States, from the normal cycle of electoral politics.

In Portugal, the governing Socialists won re-election on Sunday, but lost an absolute parliamentary majority. In Spain, the Socialists still get credit for opposing both Franco and the Iraq war. In Germany, the broad left, including the Greens, has a structural majority in Parliament, but the Social Democrats, in postelection crisis, must contemplate allying with the hard left, Die Linke, which has roots in the old East German Communist Party.

Part of the problem is the "wall in the head" between East and West Germans. While the Christian Democrats moved smoothly eastward, the Social Democrats of the West never joined with the Communists. "The two Germanys, one Socialist, one Communist—two souls—never really merged," said Giovanni Sartori, a professor emeritus at Columbia University. "It explains why the S.P.D., which was always the major Socialist party in Europe, cannot really coalesce."

The situation in France is even worse for the left. Asked this summer if the party was dying, Bernard-Henri Lévy, an emblematic Socialist, answered: "No—it is already dead. No one, or nearly no one, dares to say it. But everyone, or nearly everyone, knows it." While he was accused of exaggerating, given that the party is the largest in opposition and remains popular in local government, his words struck home.

The Socialist Party, with a long revolutionary tradition and weakening ties to a diminishing working class, is riven by personal rivalries. The party last won the presidency in 1988, and in 2007, Ségolène Royal lost the presidency to Mr. Sarkozy by 6.1 percent, a large margin.

With a reputation for flakiness, Ms. Royal narrowly lost the party leadership election last year to a more doctrinaire Socialist, Martine Aubry, by 102 votes out of 135,000. The ensuing allegations of fraud further chilled their relations.

While Ms. Royal would like to move the Socialists to the center and explore a more formal coalition with the Greens and the Democratic Movement of François Bayrou, Ms. Aubry fears diluting the party. She is both famous and infamous for achieving the 35-hour workweek in the last Socialist government.

The French Socialist Party "is trapped in a hopeless contradiction," said Tony Judt, director of the Remarque Institute at New York University. It espouses a radical platform it cannot deliver; the result leaves space for parties to its left that can take as much as 15 percent of the vote.

Angela Merkel became chancellor of Germany in 2005. She led a coalition of her own center-right party (Christian Democratic Union), the Christian Social Union, and the Social Democratic Party of Germany. Merkel's pre-election platform supported reform of labor laws to allow more layoffs and longer hours. Some took her election as a sign of a movement away from socialism. © vario images GmbHandCo/KG/Alamy.

The party, at its summer retreat last month at La Rochelle, a coastal resort, still talked of "comrades" and "party militants." Its seminars included "Internationalism at Globalized Capitalism's Hour of Crisis."

But its infighting has drawn ridicule. Mr. Sarkozy told his party this month that he sent "a big thank-you" to Ms. Royal, "who is helping me a lot," and Daniel Cohn-Bendit, a prominent European Green politician, said "everyone has cheated" in the Socialist Party and accused Ms. Royal of acting like "an outraged young girl."

The internecine squabbling in France and elsewhere has done little to position Socialist parties to answer the question of the moment: how to preserve the welfare state amid slower growth and rising deficits. The Socialists have, in this contest, become conservatives, fighting to preserve systems that voters think need to be improved, though not abandoned.

"The Socialists can't adapt to the loss of their basic electorate, and with globalism, the welfare state can no longer exist in the same way," Professor Sartori said.

Enrico Letta, 43, is one of the hopes of Italy's left, currently in disarray in the face of Silvio Berlusconi's nationalist populism. "We have to understand that Socialism is an answer of the last century," Mr. Letta said. "We need to build a center-left that is pragmatic, that provides an attractive alternative, and not just an opposition."

Mr. Letta argues that Socialist policies will have to be transmuted into a more fluid form to allow an alliance with center, liberal and green parties that won't be called "Socialist."

Mr. Winock, the historian, said, "I think the left and Socialism in Europe still have work to do; they have a raison d'être, and they will have to rely more on environment issues." Combined with continuing efforts to reduce income disparity, he said, "going green" may give the left more life.

Mr. Judt argues that European Socialists need a new message—how to reform capitalism, "recognizing the centrality of economic interest while displacing it from its throne as the only way of talking about politics."

European Socialists need "to think a lot harder about what the state can and can't do in the 21st century," he said.

Not an easy syllabus. But without that kind of reform, Mr. Judt said, "I don't think Socialism in Europe has a future; and given that it is a core constitutive part of the European democratic consensus, that's bad news."

For Further Discussion

1. In Chapter 1, in a preface that was intended to be published with *Animal Farm* but was not included because of its challenging nature, Orwell writes about freedom of the press. He states he had a difficult time finding a publisher for *Animal Farm* because the novel was critical of the Soviet Union, an unpopular position when the Soviet Union was a wartime ally of Great Britain. What topics can you think of that are unpopular to write about today? Do you believe, as Orwell did, that freedom of the press should be absolute? Give reasons for your opinion.

2. In Chapter 1, John P. Rossi writes that Orwell remains relevant in the twenty-first century. Rossi cites two Orwell themes as especially relevant today—a fear that history would become the story of totalitarian regimes endlessly engaged in conflict and that truth would become obscured by propaganda. Do you find these themes relevant today? What examples can you cite from current history to support your view?

3. In Chapter 2, Averil Gardner writes that while *Animal Farm* is satirizing the Russian Revolution specifically, it has a universal message that all revolutions are doomed to failure. Do you think Orwell would agree with this statement? Why or why not? Do you agree with this statement? Why or why not? Cite specific examples from history to support your position.

4. In Chapter 2, Katharine Byrne contends that *Animal Farm* is about the tendency of power to corrupt. Byrne states that Orwell's message is that citizens are responsible for their own liberty. Do you agree with this statement? What specifics can you cite from the text of *Animal Farm* to

support your position? What specifics can you cite in history that demonstrate that people can successfully achieve their own liberty?

5. In Chapter 3, Cathy Young says that conservatives who are calling the Barack Obama administration socialist are simply wrong, while Jonah Goldberg argues that the United States is becoming more socialist (though he labels it technically as more fascist) under the Obama administration, while Alan Wolfe sees it as liberalism. Orwell was an avowed socialist throughout his life. Do you believe he would consider the Obama administration socialist? Why or why not?

For Further Reading

Margaret Atwood, *The Handmaid's Tale*. Toronto: McClelland and Stewart, 1985.

Ray Bradbury, *Fahrenheit 451*. New York: Ballantine Books, 1953.

Anthony Burgess, *A Clockwork Orange*. London: Heinemann, 1962.

William Golding, *Lord of the Flies*. London: Faber & Faber, 1954.

Joseph Heller, *Catch-22*. New York: Simon & Schuster, 1961.

Aldous Huxley, *Brave New World*. Garden City, NY: Doubleday, 1932.

Ken Kesey, *One Flew over the Cuckoo's Nest*. New York: Viking, 1962.

George Orwell, *The Collected Essays, Journalism and Letters of George Orwell*. Edited by Sonia Orwell and Ian Angus. London: Secker & Warburg, 1968.

———, *Down and Out in Paris and London*. New York: Harper, 1933.

———, *Nineteen Eighty-Four*. London: Secker & Warburg, 1949.

J.D. Salinger, *The Catcher in the Rye*. Boston: Little, Brown, 1951.

John Steinbeck, *Of Mice and Men*. New York: Covici Friede, 1937.

Jonathan Swift, *Gulliver's Travels*. 1726. Oxford World's Classics edition, edited by Claude Rawson and Ian Higgins. Oxford: Oxford University Press, 2008.

Kurt Vonnegut Jr., *Slaughterhouse-Five; or, The Children's Crusade: A Duty Dance with Death.* New York: Seymour Lawrence/Delacorte, 1969.

Bibliography

Books

Keith Alldritt — *The Making of George Orwell: An Essay in Literary History.* New York: St. Martin's Press, 1969.

John Atkins — *George Orwell: A Literary Study.* London: J. Calder, 1954.

David Ciepley — *Liberalism in the Shadow of Totalitarianism.* Cambridge, MA: Harvard University Press, 2006.

G.A. Cohen — *Why Not Socialism?* Princeton, NJ: Princeton University Press, 2009.

Mark Connelly — *The Diminished Self: Orwell and the Loss of Freedom.* Pittsburgh: Dusquesne University Press, 1987.

Audrey Coppard and Bernard Crick — *Orwell Remembered.* London: British Broadcasting Corp., 1984.

Bernard Crick — *George Orwell: A Life.* Boston: Little, Brown, 1980.

Thomas Cushman and John Rodden, eds. — *George Orwell into the Twenty-First Century.* Boulder, CO: Paradigm, 2004.

Peter Davison — *George Orwell: A Literary Life.* New York: St. Martin's Press, 1996.

T.R. Fyvel   *George Orwell.* New York: Macmillan, 1982.

Miriam Gross, ed.   *The World of George Orwell.* London: Weidenfeld and Nicolson, 1971.

Christopher   *A Study of George Orwell.* New York:
Hollis   St. Martin's Press, 1995.

Stephen Ingle   *George Orwell: A Political Life.* New York: Manchester University Press, 1993.

David Kubal   *Outside the Whale: George Orwell's Art and Politics.* South Bend, IN: University of Notre Dame Press, 1972.

Michael A.   *Build It Now: Socialism for the*
Lebowitz   *Twenty-First Century.* New York: Monthly Review Press, 2006.

Alan Maass   *The Case for Socialism.* Chicago: Haymarket Books, 2005.

Joseph A.   *Capitalism, Socialism and Democracy.*
Schumpeter   Oxford, UK: Routledge Classics, 2010.

Michael Shelden   *Orwell: The Authorized Biography.* New York: HarperCollins, 1991.

Peter Stansky   *The Unknown Orwell.* New York:
and William   Knopf, 1972.
Abrahams

Lionel Trilling "George Orwell and the Politics of Truth." In *The Opposing Self: Nine Essays in Criticism.* New York: Viking, 1955.

Richard J. Voorhees *The Paradox of George Orwell.* West Lafayette, IN: Purdue University Press, 1986.

Raymond Williams, ed. *George Orwell: A Collection of Critical Essays.* Englewood Cliffs, NJ: Prentice-Hall, 1974.

Walter E. Williams *Liberty Versus the Tyranny of Socialism: Controversial Essays.* Stanford, CA: Hoover Institution Press, 2008.

George Woodcock *The Crystal Spirit: A Study of George Orwell.* Boston: Little, Brown, 1966.

Alex Zwerdling *Orwell and the Left.* New Haven, CT: Yale University Press, 1974.

Periodicals

W.H. Auden "George Orwell," *Spectator*, January 16, 1971.

Peter Beinart "The Good Fight," *New Republic*, December 20, 2004.

Spencer Brown "Strange Doings at *Animal Farm*," *Commentary*, February 1955.

Robert Christgau "Writing for the People," *Village Voice*, February 1, 1983.

Arthur C. Danto   *"Animal Farm* at 50," *New York Times Book Review*, April 14, 1996.

Robert M. Davis   "Politics in the Pig-Pen," *Journal of Popular Culture*, vol. 2, 1968.

R. Bruce Douglass   "The Fate of Orwell's Warning," *Thought: A Review of Culture and Idea*, September 1985.

Valerie Eliot   "T.S. Eliot and *Animal Farm*: Reason for Rejection," *Times* (London), June 6, 1969.

Christopher Hitchens and Norman Podhoretz   "An Exchange on Orwell," *Harper's Magazine*, February 1983.

Anthony Kearney   "Orwell's *Animal Farm* and *1984*," *Explicator*, Summer 1996.

Mark Leibovich   "'Socialism!' Boo, Hiss, Repeat," *New York Times*, February 28, 2009.

Harold Meyerson   "Who You Calling Socialist?" *Washington Post*, March 4, 2009.

Dick Morris   "The Obama Presidency: Here Comes Socialism," Real Clear Politics, January 21, 2009. www.realclearpolitics.com/articles/2009/01/the_obama_presidency_here_come.html.

Michael Peter   "*Animal Farm* Fifty Years On," *Contemporary Review*, August 1995.

Norman   "If Orwell Were Alive Today,"
Podhoretz   *Harper's Magazine*, January 1983.

V.S. Pritchett   "George Orwell," *New Statesman and Nation*, January 28, 1950.

Philip Rieff   "George Orwell and the Post-liberal Imagination," *Kenyon Review*, Winter 1954.

John Rodden   "George Orwell; Pickwickian Radical? An Ambivalent Case," *Kenyon Review*, Summer 1990.

Andre Schiffrin   "Socialism Is No Longer a Dirty Word," *Nation*, December 29, 2008.

Tzvetan Todorov   "Politics, Morality, and the Writer's Life: Notes on George Orwell," *Stanford French Review*, vol. 16, no. 1, 1992.

Index

A

Allegory
  Animal Farm as political, 54–
    65, 83–86, 108–111, 118–
    119, 143–148
  of common people, 78
  meanings in, 115
  of revolution, 80
  use of animals for, 105
Allied Forces, 12
Anglo-Russian Treaty, 76
Animal fable, 56, 61–62, 83–87,
  95–100, 118, 147
Animal Farm (Orwell)
  adaptations of, *49, 68, 87, 98*
  ambiguity in, 116–124
  as animal story, 82–83, 85
  circular construction of, 131,
    137
  contemporary relevance of,
    45, 89–91, 102, 128–129
  difficulty in publishing, 11–12,
    31, 34–44, 77–78, 88, 125
  distorts Russian history, 66–70
  emotional power of, 104–108,
    115
  erroneous view of Commu-
    nism in, 71–74
  as fable, 86–87, 91, 95
  genre of, 55–56, 83, 97–100
  historical context for, 11–14,
    81–91
  humor in, 117–118
  lack of narrator in, 101–102
  language in, 62–63, 99–100,
    134, 138–139
  literary devices in, 60–63

  misunderstandings of, 87–89
  moral of, 121–122
  notion of liberty in, 111–114
  as parable, 148–149
  plot of, 30–31
  as political allegory, 54–65, 80,
    83–86, 108–111, 118–119,
    143–148
  Russian history represented
    in, 58–60, 66–70, 75–76, 84–
    85, 93–94, 108, 119–122, 130
  as satire of dictatorships, 92–
    102
  as satire of revolutions, 103–
    104, 108–111, 121–122, 130–
    138, 142–143
  setting for, 106–107
  success of, 125–126
  symbolic levels of, 86–88
  symbolism in, 94
  tone of, 98–99
  view of society in, 144–146
  warning in, 21
  writing of, 117
Animal imagery, 96, 146–147
Animalism, 106, 111, 131
Animals
  cultural stereotypes of, 83–84
  exploitation of, 85–86
  Orwell's love and knowledge
    of, 95–97, 105–106, 118
  realistic presentation of, 105–
    106, 118
Aubry, Martine, 169
Autobiographical work, 22, 23, 26